teach® yourself

buying a home in portugal

peter and nat macbride

with bill and isa reed

teach yourself®

buying a home in portugal

peter and nat macbride

with bill and isa reed

for over 60 years, more than 40 million people have learnt over 750 subjects the **teach yourself** way, with impressive results

be where you want to be with **teach yourself**

For UK order enquiries: please contact Bookpoint Ltd, 130 Milton Park, Abingdon, Oxon OX14 4SB. Telephone: +44 (0)1235 827720. Fax: +44 (0)1235 400454. Lines are open 09.00–18.00, Monday to Saturday, with a 24-hour message answering service. Details about our titles and how to order are available at www.teachyourself.co.uk.

Long renowned as the authoritative source for self-guided learning – with more than 40 million copies sold worldwide – the **teach yourself** series includes over 300 titles in the fields of languages, crafts, hobbies, business, computing and education.

British Library Cataloguing in Publication Data: a catalogue record for this title is available from The British Library.

First published in UK 2005 by Hodder Education, 338 Euston Road, London, NW1 3BH.

The **teach yourself** name is a registered trade mark of Hodder Headline

Computer hardware and software brand names mentioned in this book are protected by their respective trademarks and are acknowledged.

Text and photographs copyright © 2005 Peter MacBride and Nat MacBride

Drawn illustrations copyright © 2005 Art Construction

In UK: All rights reserved. Apart from any permitted use under UK copyright law, no part of this publication may be reproduced or transmitted in any form or by any means, electronic or mechanical, including photocopy, recording, or any information, storage and retrieval system, without permission in writing from the publisher or under licence from the Copyright Licensing Agency Limited. Further details of such licences (for reprographic reproduction) may be obtained from the Copyright Licensing Agency Limited, of 90 Tottenham Court Road, London W1T 4LP.

Typeset by MacDesign, Southampton

Printed in Great Britain for Hodder Education, a division of Hodder Headline, 338 Euston Road, London NW1 3BH by Cox & Wyman Ltd, Reading, Berkshire.

Hodder Headline's policy is to use papers that are natural, renewable and recyclable products and made from wood grown in sustainable forests. The logging and manufacturing processes are expected to conform to the environmental regulations of the country of origin.

Impression number	10 9 8 7 6 5 4 3 2 1
Year	2009 2008 2007 2006 2005

contents

	preface	ix
01	**a pesquisa – the search**	**1**
	Almost the same…	2
	Define your search	2
	Searching through the web	5
	Os agentes imobiliários – estate agents	9
	Search on the ground	15
	New houses	16
	Inspection tours	17
	Lexicon: a pesquisa – the search	18
	Agente imobiliário abbreviations	20
	Lexicon: os tipos de vivendas – types of property	20
	Lexicon: as divisões e as características – rooms and features	21
	Found it?	23
	English – Portuguese quick reference	24
02	**a venda – the sale**	**28**
	Almost the same…	29
	A propriedade e a lei – ownership and the law	30
	A compra duma propriedade nova – buying a new property	32
	A oferta de compra – the purchase offer	32
	O contrato de promessa de compra e venda – the sale contract	33

	Lexicon: o contrato – the contract	36
	Finance	37
	A escritura – the deed of sale	39
	Fees and charges	40
	Lexicon: a venda – the sale	41
	Os serviços – services	42
	Lexicon: os serviços – services	43
	English – Portuguese quick reference	44
03	**as obras – building work**	**46**
	Almost the same…	47
	Check at the câmara (town hall)	47
	PDM – the town planning brief	48
	A licença de obras – the building permit	48
	As obras e os construtores – the building and builders	49
	Lexicon: as obras – building work	51
	English – Portuguese quick reference	52
04	**a estrutura – the structure**	**53**
	Almost the same…	54
	Check at the câmara	55
	A estrutura – the structure	55
	O telhado – the roofing	56
	A cobertura – roofing materials	58
	As paredes – walls	59
	Os tectos e os chãos – ceilings and floors	64
	English – Portuguese quick reference	65
05	**a carpintaria – woodwork**	**70**
	Almost the same…	71
	Check at the câmara	71
	A carpintaria interna – internal woodwork	72
	As portas – doors	73
	As janelas – windows	75
	As persianas – shutters	76
	A escada – staircase	78
	Os armários e as prateleiras – cupboards and shelves	79

	A madeira – wood	79
	As ferramentas – tools	80
	English – Portuguese quick reference	83
06	**a canalização – plumbing**	**89**
	Almost the same…	90
	Check at the câmara	91
	A canalização – pipework	91
	A casa de banho – the bathroom	94
	A cozinha – kitchen	98
	A fossa séptica – the septic tank	100
	As ferramentas – tools	102
	English – Portuguese quick reference	103
07	**o aquecimento e a electricidade – heating and electricity**	**107**
	Almost the same…	108
	O aquecimento – heating	108
	Lexicon: o aquecimento – heating	111
	O abastecimento de electricidade – the electricity supply	113
	Os electrodomésticos – electrical appliances	116
	A iluminação – lighting	118
	As ferramentas – tools	119
	English – Portuguese quick reference	120
08	**a decoração – decorating**	**124**
	Almost the same…	125
	Check at the câmara	125
	A pintura – paint	125
	Os revestimentos de paredes – wall coverings	127
	As cortinas e os estores – curtains and blinds	131
	Os móveis – furniture	132
	English – Portuguese quick reference	134
09	**o jardim – the garden**	**138**
	Almost the same…	139
	Check at the câmara	140
	As cercas – walls, fences and hedges	140
	A piscina – the swimming pool	141

	Os móveis do jardim – garden furniture	143
	A jardinagem – gardening	144
	As ferramentas – tools	145
	English – Portuguese quick reference	147
10	**uma hora de português – an hour of Portuguese**	**151**
	The CD and the book	152
	Speaking and listening	152
	Gender and endings	155
	Verbs	156
	Greetings	160
	Asking questions	160
	A pesquisa – the search	162
	A venda – the sale	164
	As obras – building work	166
	A estrutura – the structure	167
	A carpintaria – woodwork	169
	A canalização – plumbing	171
	O aquecimento e a electricidade – heating and electricity	172
	A decoração – decorating	174
	O jardim – the garden	176

preface

The thought behind this book is a simple one. If you want to buy a house in Portugal, it helps if you know the words. This isn't the same as being able to speak Portuguese – even with a degree in Portuguese, you won't necessarily know your *escritura* (deed of sale) from your *beiral* (eaves). No, you don't actually have to be able to speak Portuguese – though it helps no end if you do – but if you know the words that describe houses and their various components, and the words that are involved in the sale process, then you will be better equipped for finding, buying and settling into your Portuguese home.

Buying a Home in Portugal covers around 750 of the most useful words for house buyers, but this book is not a dictionary. A translation alone is sometimes not enough. It doesn't get you very much further to know that *notário* translates to 'notary', or that *beiral* means 'eaves'. You need to know what the *notário*'s role is and how it affects you, and where the *beiral* are to be found. The words are given here in the context of the buying process or of different aspects of the house. Where it will help, we have explained the concepts behind the words or given an illustration.

We couldn't have produced this book without the assistance of our collaborators, Bill and Isa Reed of Casa das Oliveiras (www.casa-das-oliveiras.com). Thanks are also due to Sue Hart and Ginny Catmur of Hodder and Stoughton, Mike Hayes of Homes Overseas, Tony Jones of Art Construction and Jake McBride, our UK building expert.

Peter and Nat MacBride

The CD

The CD that accompanies this book is designed to be used alongside Chapter 10, *Uma hora de português – an hour of Portuguese*. There are 20 tracks:

Track 1 is a brief introduction to the Portuguese language, covering pronunciation, how to greet people, ask questions and understand simple replies.

The remaining tracks all give practice in speaking and listening to some of the most important or useful words in each chapter. It should take between 5 and 15 minutes to complete each one – work through a track before going out to tackle a job and you will be better prepared to deal with the *agentes* and the *construtores*.

Track 2 links to Chapter 1, *A pesquisa – the search*

Track 3 links to Chapter 2, *A venda – the sale*

Track 4 links to Chapter 3, *As obras – building work*

Tracks 5–7 link to Chapter 4, *A estrutura – the structure*

Track 5: *Talking to o construtor – the builder*

Track 6: *Finding tools and materials at the bricolagem*

Track 7: *Talking to o carpinteiro and o telhador – the carpenter and the roofer*

Tracks 8–10 link to Chapter 5, *A carpinteria – woodwork*

Track 8: *Talking to o carpinteiro – the joiner*

Track 9: *Finding materials at the bricolagem*

Track 10: *Finding tools at the bricolagem*

Tracks 11–13 link to Chapter 6, *A canalização – plumbing*

Track 11: *Talking to o canalizador – the plumber*

Track 12: *Shopping for bathroom and kitchen equipment*

Track 13: *Finding tools at the bricolagem*

Tracks 14–15 link to Chapter 7, *O aquecimento e a electricidade – heating and electricity*

Track 14: *Talking to o engenheiro do aquecimento and o electricista – the heating engineer and the electrician*

Track 15: *Shopping for os electrodomésticos – electrical appliances*

Tracks 16–18 link to Chapter 8, *A decoração – decorating*

Track 16: *Finding materials at the bricolagem*

Track 17: *Finding tools at the bricolagem*

Track 18: *Finding floor coverings, curtains and furniture*

Tracks 19–20 link to Chapter 9, *O jardim – the garden*

Track 19: *Talking to os construtores – the builders*

Track 20: *Shopping for o jardim – the garden*

The voices on the CD are those of Maria Lima and Stuart Nurse.

01
a pesquisa – the search

Almost the same...

In Portugal as in the UK, property is usually sold through *agentes imobiliários* (estate agents), though private sales are more common than here. You might see *vende-se* or *à venda* (for sale) signs attached to gate posts or in windows. This may reflect the high rates of commission charged by Portuguese estate agents – generally from 5 to 10%. Portuguese agents have to be licensed and should have a certificate displayed somewhere to show they are a *mediador autorizado* (authorised agent). As might be expected in a market with such tidy profits there are cowboys about, so make sure you look for agents who are registered with a professional body such as AMI (*Associação de Mediadores Imobiliários*) or SMI (*Sociedade de Mediação Imobiliária*).

Once you get there, Portuguese agents are much the same as those in the UK. The main difference is that you won't be set upon the moment you set foot inside! Agents will have information (of varying quality) on hand, and will be happy to arrange visits for you. They will accompany you on the viewing – it's rare that the vendor will have to show you round their own house. The willingness (and ability) of an *agente* to help ranges from the useless to those who really know their properties well, and take the time to find out what you are really after. If you're out in Portugal on a buying trip, you don't have time to waste on the first kind. It's better to spend time up front finding a good agent than driving around viewing unsuitable properties suggested by a bad one.

Define your search

Where do you want to buy? In which region? In a big town, a village, an *urbanização* (purpose-built development) or rural isolation? Beach or mountains? What sort and size of property do you want? A flat, a small cottage or a plush villa? Do you want a garden or a terrace? What about a pool – private or communal? How much work do you want to have to do on it? Are you looking for a ruin to rebuild, an old house to restore, one that needs a little light redecorating, or a new build?

These are questions that only you can answer – this checklist may help you to define your ideal house.

Ideal house checklist

Location: Province or region ....
Beach, mountains or other? ....
City, village, *urbanização* or countryside? ....
Is the view important? ....
Max distance from airport ....
Max distance from shops ....
Max distance from cafés/restaurants ....
Max distance from beach/swimming/etc. ....
Max distance from children's play facilities ....

Size: Number of bedrooms ....
Other rooms ....
Minimum total floorspace (1) ....

Outside: Swimming pool? (None/Communal/Private) ......
Garage/parking needed? (Y/N) ....
Garden/land? (None/Communal/Private) ....
Minimum garden/land area ....

Condition: New build, or resale? (2) ....
Ruin/renovation/redecoration/ready? (3) ....
What furniture/fittings are present? ....

Budget: How much money is available? ....
How much time do you have (4) ....

(1) The size of a house is normally expressed in total floor area. A cottage or small terraced house is around 50m², 100m² is equivalent to a typical new British semi, 200m² is the size of an older 5-bed detached house in the UK.

(2) Fees and taxes will add approx 5% to the cost of a new house and 10-15% to the cost of a resale (see page 40).

(3) If you plan to rebuild or restore, you must have some idea of the cost of building work and be prepared to deal with the paperwork (see Chapter 3).

(4) The less time you have to work on the house, the more professional services you will have to buy.

The provinces

1. Algarve
2. Alto Alentejo
3. Baixo Alentejo
4. Beira Alta
5. Beira Baixa
6. Beira Litoral
7. Douro Litoral
8. Estremadura
9. Minho
10. Ribatejo
11. Trás-os-Montes

The Algarve (below) is by far the best-known and most popular part of Portugal, but it is not the only province. The sweeping Atlantic coasts and the spectacular mountains should not be ignored.

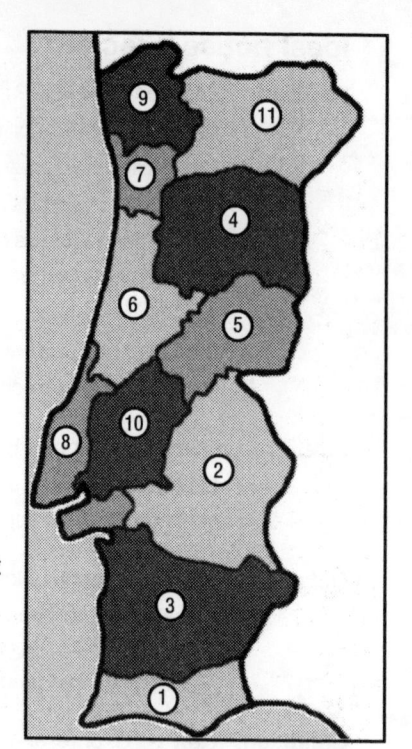

The Algarve

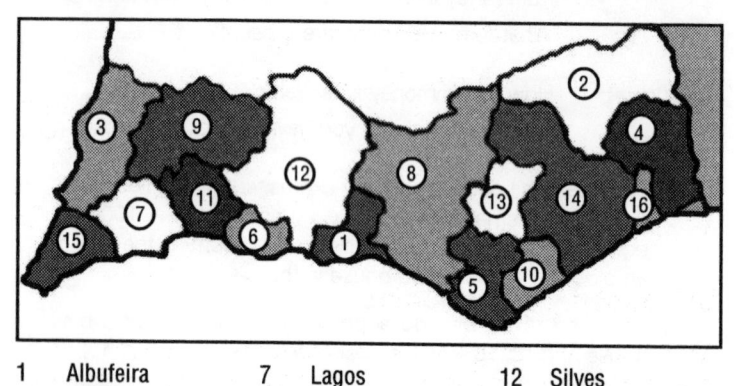

1. Albufeira
2. Alcoutim
3. Aljezur
4. Castro Marim
5. Faro
6. Lagoa
7. Lagos
8. Loulé
9. Monchique
10. Olhão
11. Portimão
12. Silves
13. S. Brás
14. Tavira
15. Vila do Bispo
16. V. Real

> If you don't know where you want to be, or what sort of house, spend more time exploring Portugal, renting different types of houses in different areas, then start looking.

Searching through the web

Get online before you leave home and give yourself a head start. You may be able to find your house through the web but even if you don't find a specific one, you will find the more active agents and get a good idea of the prices and the kind of properties available in an area.

If you miss out the web search, you will spend the first days of your visit hunting through the *Páginas Amarelas* (Yellow Pages) or the town itself looking for the *agentes imobiliários*.

If you're looking for a new-build home in an *urbanização*, you are probably best going to a UK-based site, since the *urbanizações* are built mainly for foreign owners. If you're looking for an older property in a town or in the countryside, find a Portuguese agent. Some UK agents do offer these, but will probably have a limited range, and you are less likely to pick up a bargain – these sites are aimed at well-heeled foreigners, after all.

UK vs Portuguese sites

If you are looking in the Algarve or around Lisbon, you will almost certainly find a number of UK-based agents operating in that area. Further north and inland there is less demand from foreign buyers, so fewer agents are active there. If you're looking for somewhere off the beaten track, you should go native – see the section on *agentes imobiliários* below.

UK-based property sites

As well as advertising houses, these offer varying levels of help with buying and settling in, e.g. arranging mortgages, translating legal documents, linking with English-speaking craftsmen. The main limitation, of course, is that they only have a tiny proportion of the houses on the market – most UK-based agents specialise in a particular area or work only with one developer.

If you have a very clear idea of where you want to be, try typing 'property', 'Portugal' and the name of the place into a search engine. If the type of property and location is more important than a specific place, try looking on an 'umbrella' site – one which deals with properties from many different agents. Portuguese agents tend to be quite regionally focused – if you want to get an idea of what's available across the whole of the country, you'll need to go to an umbrella site.

There is no shortage of sites dealing with Portuguese property, so set aside some time to explore the web – but to get you started, here are some UK sites that you may find useful:

- **The Move Channel** advertises properties for various agents across Portugal, providing brief details and passing requests for further information on to the relevant agent. You will need to register with them to make these requests.

    Find them at: **http://portugal.themovechannel.com**

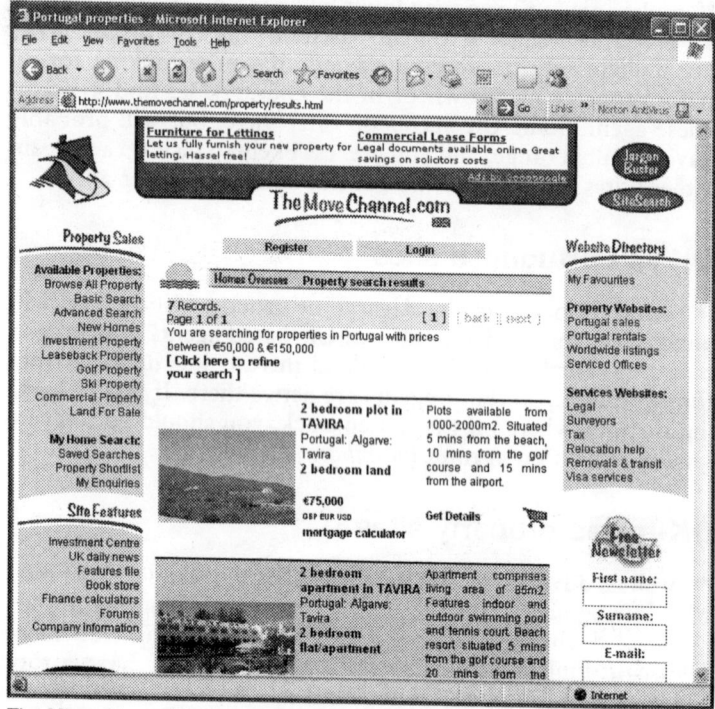

The Move Channel has properties in all price brackets – at the time of writing, the selection ranged from €45,000 to €4,000,000

- **Prestige Property** lists property details from agents throughout Portugal. As with the Move Channel, the details are not particularly thorough and you will need to register in order to request further information, but there is a good range of properties listed.

    Find them at: **http://www.prestigeproperty.co.uk** – at the top page, click on Portugal on the map.

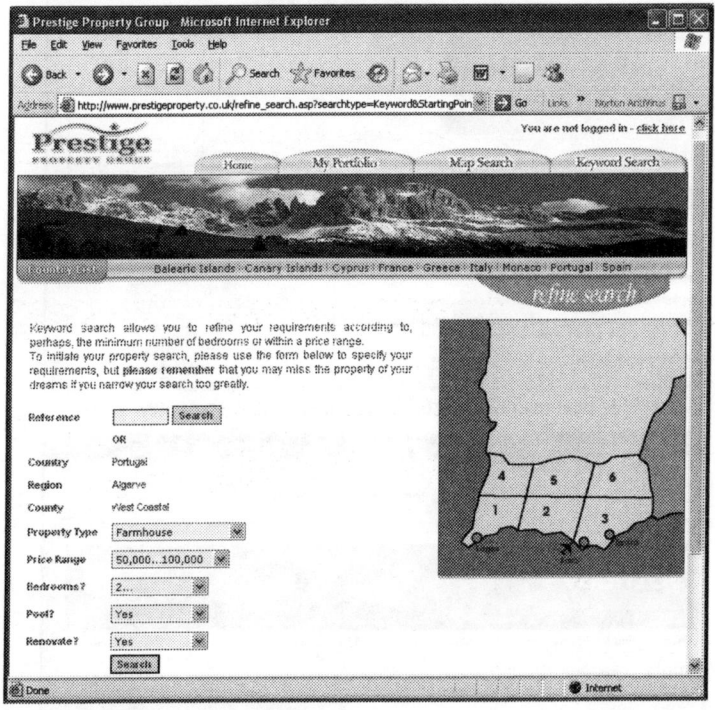

Prestige Property has an even larger choice of properties – over 600 at the time of writing – but the search form allows you to narrow this down easily.

- **Escape to Portugal** is useful if you're looking for a new-build property on an *urbanização*, as long as you're interested in the Algarve, where most of the new development takes place.

    Find them at: **http://www.escape2portugal.co.uk/**

- **Sotherby's International Realty** carries a fine selection of properties at the higher end of the market.

    Find them at: **http://www.sotherbys-realty-portugal.com**

8 a pesquisa

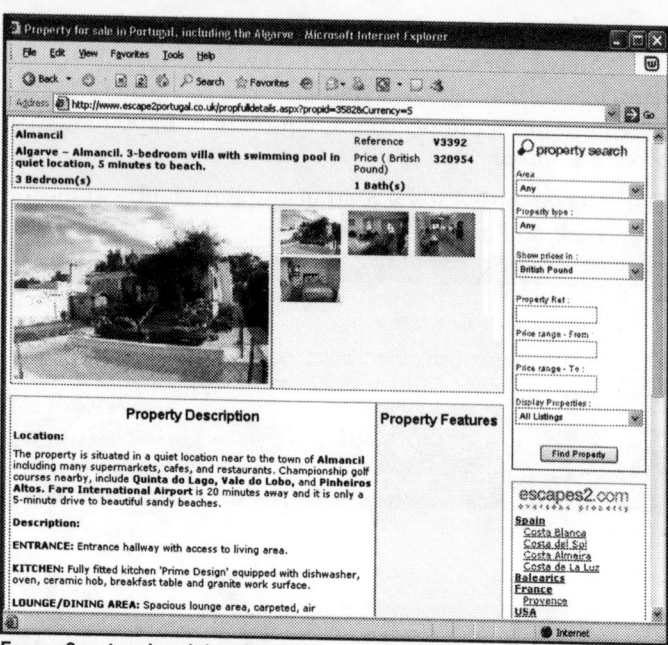

01

Escape2portugal mainly advertises apartments with some new villas.

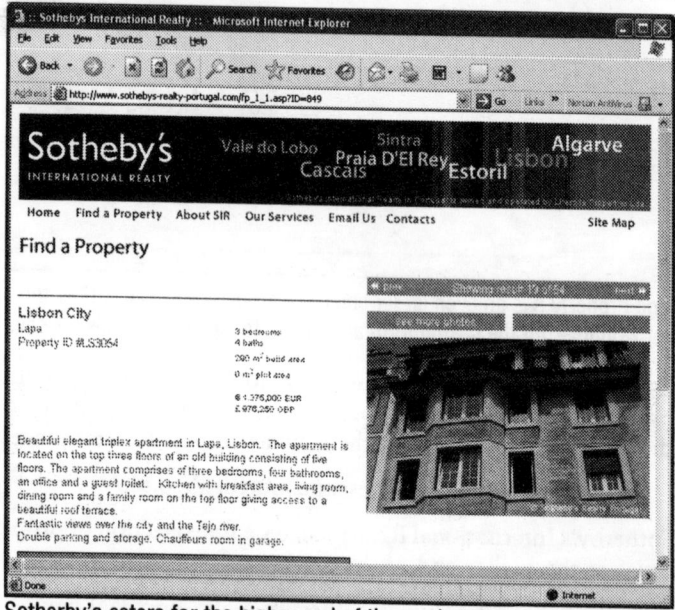

Sotherby's caters for the higher end of the market, as you might expect.

Os agentes imobiliários – estate agents

Portuguese *agentes* are usually regionally based, so you will have to go to an umbrella site to conduct any kind of nationwide search. Even then, they often require you to select specific locations before giving you a list of properties – quite frustrating if you're looking for a nice old farmhouse but don't mind where.

All the larger agents, and an increasing number of the small ones, have web sites, and most sites have a search facility. Many will have English versions, especially in the ever-popular Algarve. The searches vary, but tend to follow the same pattern – you will be asked to specify the type of property, price range and location. You may also be able to filter the selection by specifying other options such as the size (floor space in square metres), the number of rooms or whether the house is new build (*novo*) or resale (*usado*).

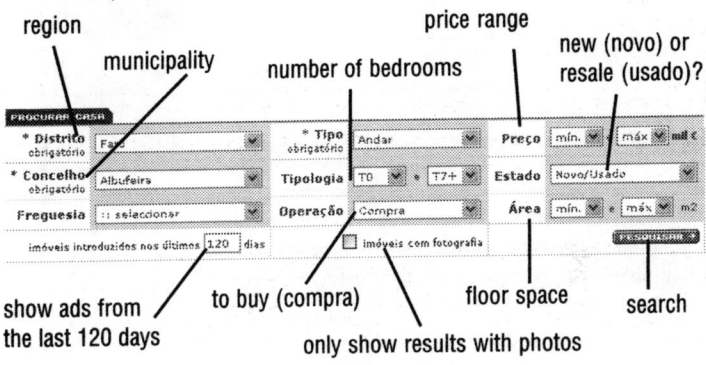

A simple search form – this is at lardocelar.com

The T number

Portuguese estate agents often refer to a property's *tipologia*, which gives ratings like T1, T2, or T5. In fact, the T number is just the number of bedrooms it has! T0 is a studio flat, and T2+1 means it has two bedrooms, plus a small box room in addition to the usual kitchen and living room. In searches, you may be asked to specify the *tipologia* you are looking for.

Not all *agentes imobiliários* have web sites, but you can still use the web to find the ones in your area. They will probably at least

a pesquisa | **10**

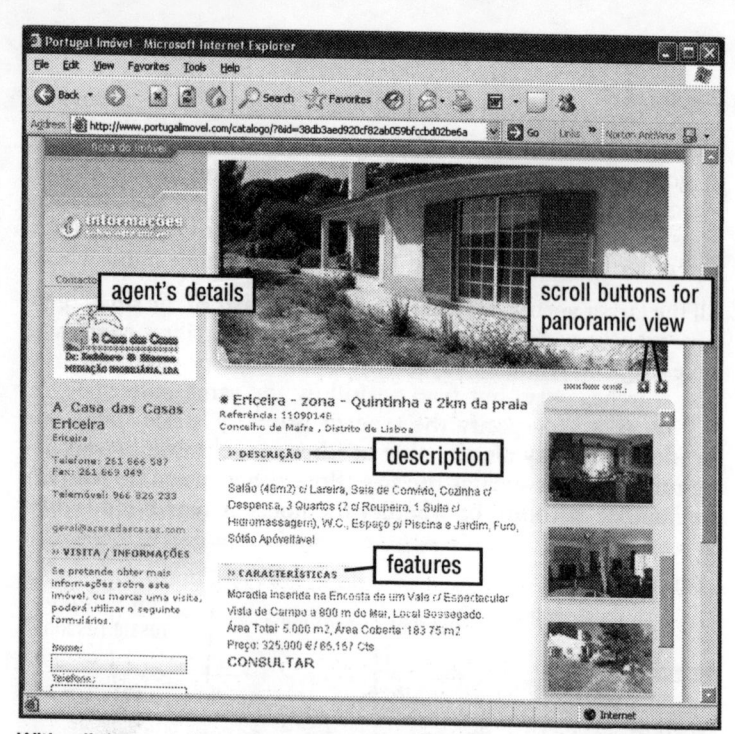

01

[Screenshot of Portugal Imóvel website with labels: "agent's details", "scroll buttons for panoramic view", "description", "features"]

With a little vocabulary you can run a search and make reasonable sense of the results at most Portuguese sites – the photos alone should give you a good guide as to whether the property is worth a closer look. This property detail page is from www.portugalimovel.com.

have an e-mail address, or you can call and speak to them directly. If you can start the conversation with *desculpe, você fala inglês?* (excuse me, do you speak English?), you'll probably get on fine!

To find a Portuguese *agente*, you can either try typing in 'imobiliário' and the name of a location you're interested in, or you can use a directory of some sort.

- Google's international directory lists a number of Portuguese agents, and manages to filter out a lot of the duff sites and broken links which plague many less thorough directories. Go to **http://directory.google.co.uk/Top/World/** and then follow the links for **Português > Regional > Europa > Portugal > Negócios e Economia > Imobiliário**

- **Sapo** (toad) is a Portuguese directory and search engine. It has hundreds of agents listed by region, though you may have to try a few before you find any really professional-looking outfits.

  Find them at **http://www.sapo.pt/empresas/imobiliarias**

There are also several umbrella sites which list agencies or offer other useful information:

- **Sapo** itself also acts as a property portal, with extensive property listings from multiple agents.

  Find them at: **http://casa.sapo.pt**

- **www.portugalimovel.com** has a good range of properties, including (at the time of writing) an old windmill in need of restoration, as well as the more usual villas and apartments. Their details are fairly brief, but more than compensated for by panoramic scrolling photos taken with a wide-angle lens.

- **www.lardocelar.com** also has lots of properties, but can be patchy on detail and photos.

- **www.imocasas.com** doesn't have a huge number of properties on its books, but carries a decent level of information about each, with links to the relevant agent's site so you can find out more. They also have a directory of property-related companies which may be of some use when you need a plumber or someone to build a swimming pool.

- Away from the Algarve, **Imobitábua** is an English-speaking, Portuguese agency based in Tábua, with a good selection of interesting properties in the green heart of Portugal.

  Find them at **www.imobitabua.com**

- **Vivencasa** is an English-speaking agency site based on the Atlantic coast between Lisbon and Porto.

  Their web site is at **http://sledgehammer.imoguia.com/**

You can usually get more information from browsing the Portuguese sites than from a single agent geared to selling its own properties to UK buyers. Of course, there is a problem with this – it will all be in Portuguese! Help is at hand though, in the form of the Google translator. This will produce an English version of any page – and only slightly garbled! (see pages 14–15).

Two properties from Imobitábua. **Top**: An old house of schist stone, in need of substantial restoration. It's in a protected village, so any rebuilding must be done in accordance with local regulations. **Bottom**: A ruin for renovation. With this you also get stables and some land with vines and fruit trees.

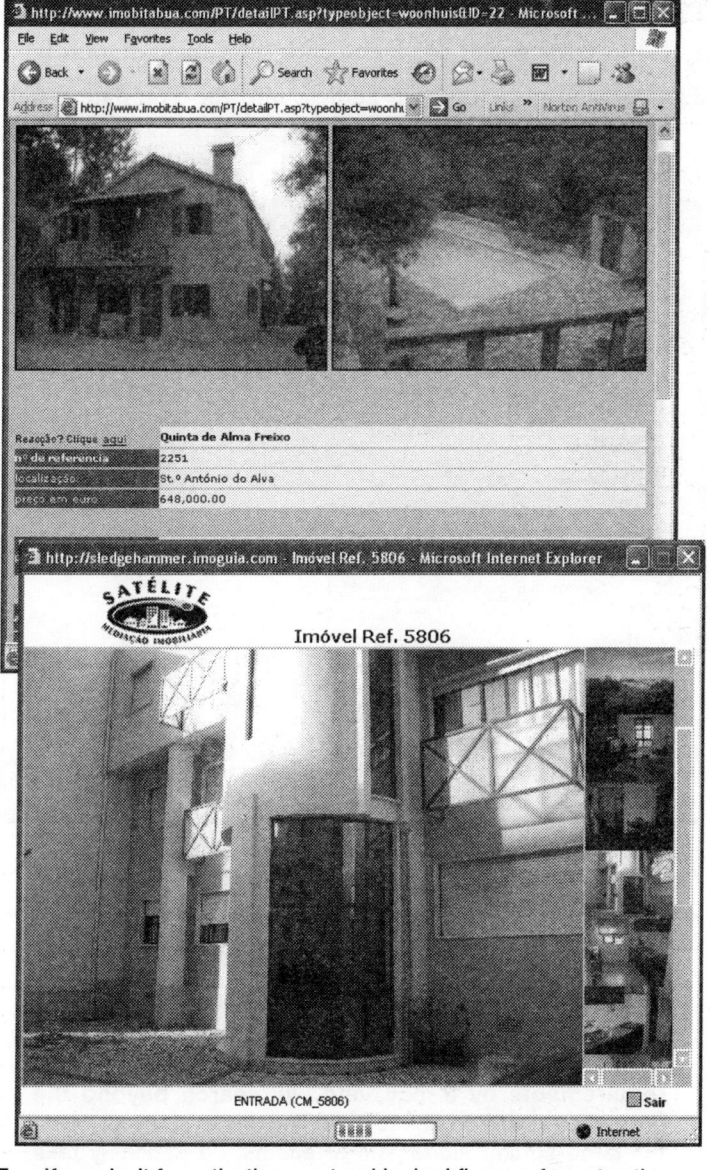

Top: If you don't fancy the time, cost and bruised fingers of a restoration project, how about this lovely granite mansion on a hill – nice views from the pool! **Bottom**: Or you could have this good sized two-bed apartment in Lisbon for just over €125,000.

To use the Google translator:

1 Go to **www.google.co.uk** and click the **Language tools** link.
2 Copy and paste the web address into the **Translate a web page** box.
3 Select **Portuguese to English** and hit **Translate**.

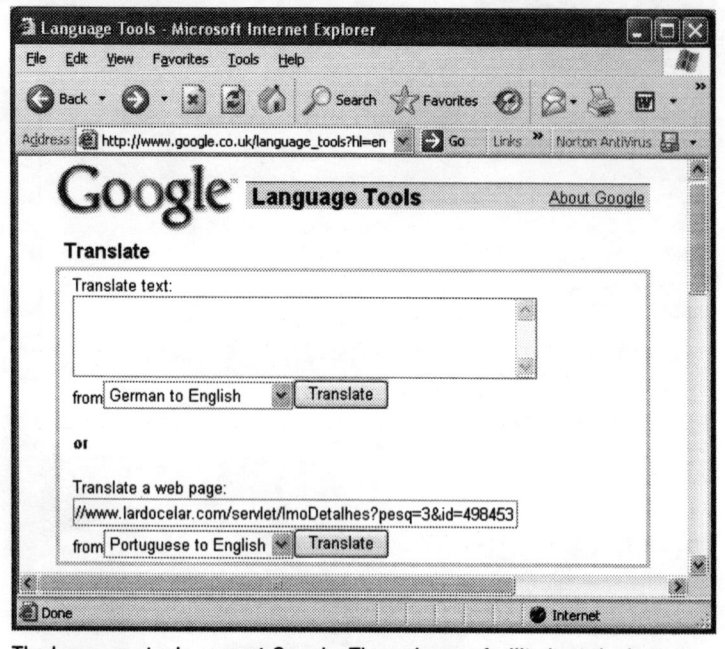

The Language tools page at Google. The web page facility is at the bottom. You can also translate text by copying and pasting it into the top box.

Agents as searchers

Some agents offer e-mail update services, that will compare your search against new properties and alert you to any that may be suitable. Others will invite you to send your requirements by e-mail, and will search beyond the properties visible on-line to try to find one to suit you. Given the large commissions paid to agents, I'd definitely take advantage of these services where you can – make them earn their money! – especially if you are short of time for searching on the ground.

| BEGINNING | SERVICES | TO LOOK HOUSE | PURCHASES |

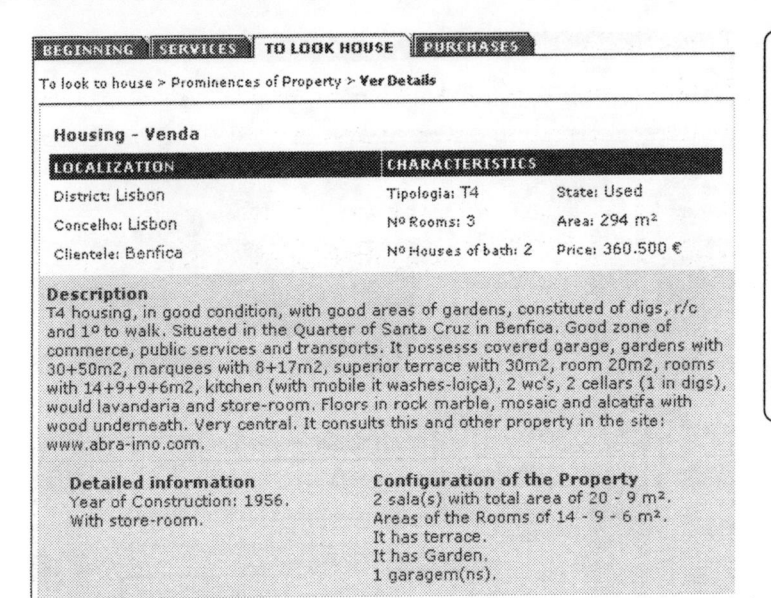

To look to house > Prominences of Property > **Ver Details**

Housing - Venda

LOCALIZATION	CHARACTERISTICS	
District: Lisbon	Tipologia: T4	State: Used
Concelho: Lisbon	Nº Rooms: 3	Area: 294 m²
Clientele: Benfica	Nº Houses of bath: 2	Price: 360.500 €

Description
T4 housing, in good condition, with good areas of gardens, constituted of digs, r/c and 1º to walk. Situated in the Quarter of Santa Cruz in Benfica. Good zone of commerce, public services and transports. It possesss covered garage, gardens with 30+50m2, marquees with 8+17m2, superior terrace with 30m2, room 20m2, rooms with 14+9+9+6m2, kitchen (with mobile it washes-loiça), 2 wc's, 2 cellars (1 in digs), would lavandaria and store-room. Floors in rock marble, mosaic and alcatifa with wood underneath. Very central. It consults this and other property in the site: www.abra-imo.com.

Detailed information
Year of Construction: 1956.
With store-room.

Configuration of the Property
2 sala(s) with total area of 20 - 9 m².
Areas of the Rooms of 14 - 9 - 6 m².
It has terrace.
It has Garden.
1 garagem(ns).

The result of a Google translation – not great literature, but you can generally understand the meaning (though 'with mobile it washes-loiça' left us scratching our heads!)

Search on the ground

When you plan your buying trip, allow at least twice as much time as you think is really necessary. Delays can happen, and if everything does goes smoothly, you can relax and treat the rest of your stay as a simple holiday.

If you found potential houses on the web, contact the *agentes imobiliários* by e-mail or phone to arrange to visit them. Allow plenty of time for each visit. The agencies may have other properties – newly-in or not advertised online – that you may want to see, and each house viewing can take a while.

Use the *Páginas Amarelas* (Yellow Pages) directory to find the other local agents and *notário* and see what they have to offer. And keep an eye out for *vende-se* or *à venda* (for sale) signs outside houses.

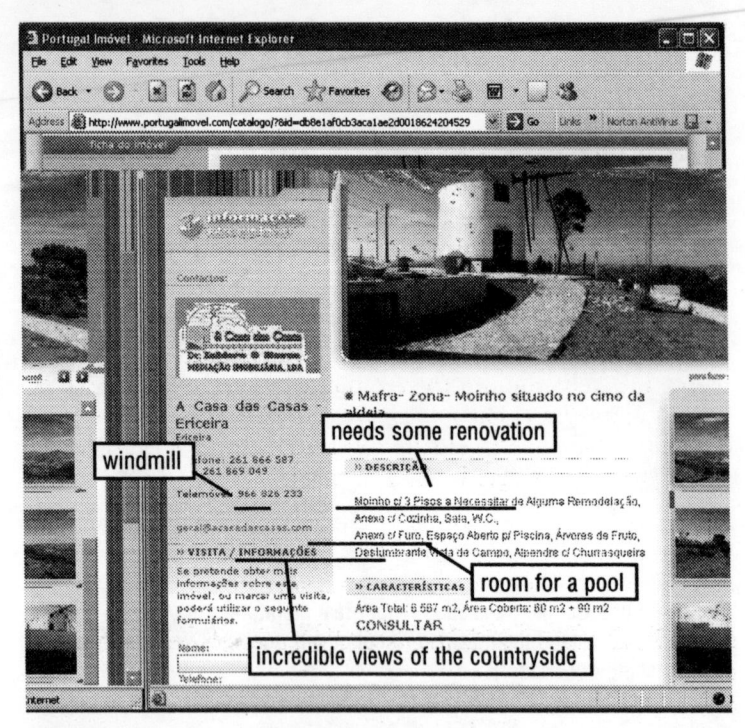

Here's an interesting restoration project for someone keen – 3 storeys of windmill on top of a hill, in need of 'some renovation'

New houses

Renovating an ancient old farmhouse is not everybody's idea of fun. New houses have nice fitted kitchens and sparkling bathrooms; they will be freshly painted and decorated throughout to your specifications; and if you have been involved from an early enough stage, the layout and the number, size and types of rooms may have been customised to your liking. And, of course, if you start from scratch with a plot of land and your own builder, then the house will be exactly as you want it (if all goes to plan…).

New houses should have guarantees on electrical and structural work, and there are some financial advantages to buying a new home. There is no property transfer tax to pay (which ranges from 0 to 8% on resale properties). New houses are subject to VAT, but this should be included in the price – ask if the price quoted includes IVA (*Imposto de Valor Acrescentado*).

Inspection tours

Most Portuguese property sites and *agentes imobiliários* deal with new houses as well as old ones, but there are of course those UK-based agents who specialise in new builds. This kind of agent will frequently offer the infamous inspection tour – a subsidised trip to Portugal to see show homes, where you will face varying degrees of pressure to sign on the dotted line before you go home.

Reputable firms won't push too hard – they know that the trips pay off their investment anyway, and the less they bully you, the more likely you are to recommend them to your friends. They'll slap 'Hurry! Only a few villas left!' notices all over their brochures, but won't actually twist your arm *too* hard when you're over in Portugal looking at them.

Others will bombard you with commission-hungry reps who will do absolutely everything they can to get you committed, and we sincerely hope you do not find yourself on such a tour. If

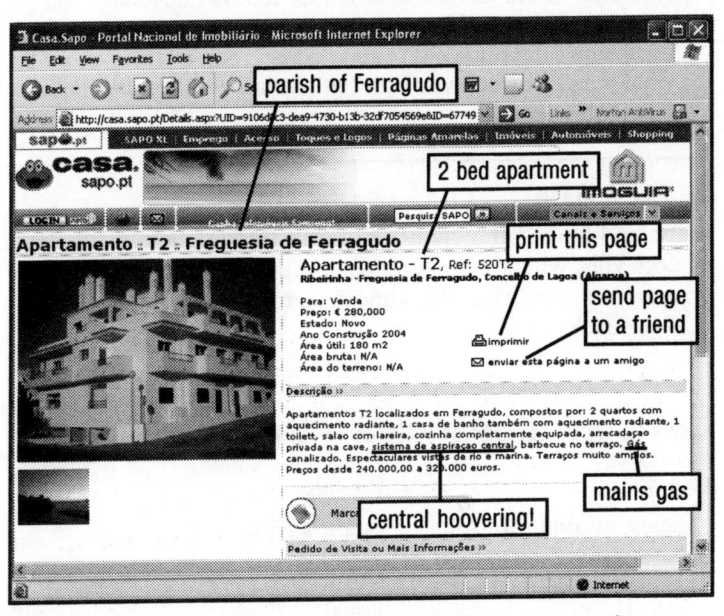

And at the other end of the scale from the windmill, here's a swanky apartment (with a built-in hoovering system, see page 18) in a new development overlooking the marina

Central hoovering

You might have noticed in the advertisement on page 17 that the property boasted a *sistema de aspiração central*. At first we thought this must have been a typo, but a little research has revealed an intriguing 'breakthrough' in home hygiene. Not content with cyclonic widgets to replace hoover bags, some brave pioneers at the cutting edge of vacuum cleaner technology have invented *aspiração central* – yes, central vacuuming!

A powerful vacuum cleaner sits out of sight in a service basement somewhere, with multiple pipes running off between floor and ceiling and inside the walls. These spread out around the house and end in hoover sockets. Simply plug in your nozzle and the machine starts sucking. No heavy equipment to lug around with you or clutter up your cupboards, just the nozzle. And apparently it's very quiet too, since the actual machine is not in the room with you.

Welcome to the wonderful world of central hoovering. You can find out more about it at the website www.selma-aspir.com. Unfortunately, the site doesn't say anything about what happens when you accidentally hoover up your wife's diamond studs...

you do, hold firm and don't do anything until you are back home and have had a chance to think calmly about it all. That perfect villa which is apparently about to be sold under your nose to someone else will almost certainly still be there when you get back.

Lexicon: a pesquisa – the search

à venda	for sale
agente imobiliário (m)	estate agent
anterior	previous
casa (f)	house
compra (f)	purchase

comprar	to buy
divisão (f)	room
moderno	modern
necessita remodelação	needs renovating
nova pesquisa (f)	new search
novo	new build
pesquisa (f)	search
pesquisar	to search
seguinte	next
terreno (m)	land
venda (f)	sale
vende-se	for sale

Buying for investment?

Some people do buy houses in Portugal more as investments than for their own use, hoping for capital growth or rental income or both. If this is your plan, you should be aware of the following: house prices have gone up significantly in recent years, as they have in the UK – and partly fuelled by the UK rises – but that is no guarantee that they will continue to do so.

Some areas of Portugal are facing serious water shortages in the near future as its tourist areas continue to expand and multiply, with thirsty golf courses, gardens and swimming pools to supply. This may threaten the rental market – or strengthen it, if restrictions are placed on new building instead of on water usage.

Then there are of course the difficulties of managing a property from afar – what happens when things break and need fixing? How far do you trust the letting agents? Can you cover the costs during periods without guests/tenants?

Think very hard, and get independent professional financial advice, before buying a property in Portugal as an investment.

Agente imobiliário abbreviations

a/c	ar condicionado	air conditioning
and	andar	storey – e.g. $5^{\underline{o}}$ and = 5th storey
apto	apartamento	apartment
aquec	aquecimento	central heating
ass	assoalhada	rooms (excluding bathroom and kitchen)
c/	com	with
coz	cozinha	kitchen
elev	elevador	lift
p/	para	for
r/c	rés de chão	ground floor
rem	remodelado	refurbished
sal	salão/sala	lounge
T1/T2/etc	tipologia	number of bedrooms
urb	urbanização	housing development

Lexicon: os tipos de vivendas – types of property

andar (m)	apartment
antigo	old
apartamento (m)	apartment
bom estado (m)	good condition
casa (f)	house
casa em banda (f)	terraced house
casa geminada (f)	semi-detached
casa individual (f)	detached house
com/sem luz	with/without electricity
com vista do mar/da serra	facing the sea/mountains
empreendimento (m)	housing development
lote (m)	building plot

moinho (m)	mill
moradia (f)	house (usually detached)
moradia rústica (f)	country house
óptimo para investimento	ideal investment
perto do mar	near the sea
quinta (f)	farmhouse
remodelado	refurbished
ruina (f)	ruin – expect to knock it down and start from scratch
rústico	in the country
terreno rustico (m)	agricultural land – usually with permission to build a farmhouse
vila/vivenda (f)	villa
vistas (fpl)	(good) views
vivenda (f)	house (usually detached)

Lexicon: as divisões e as características – rooms and features

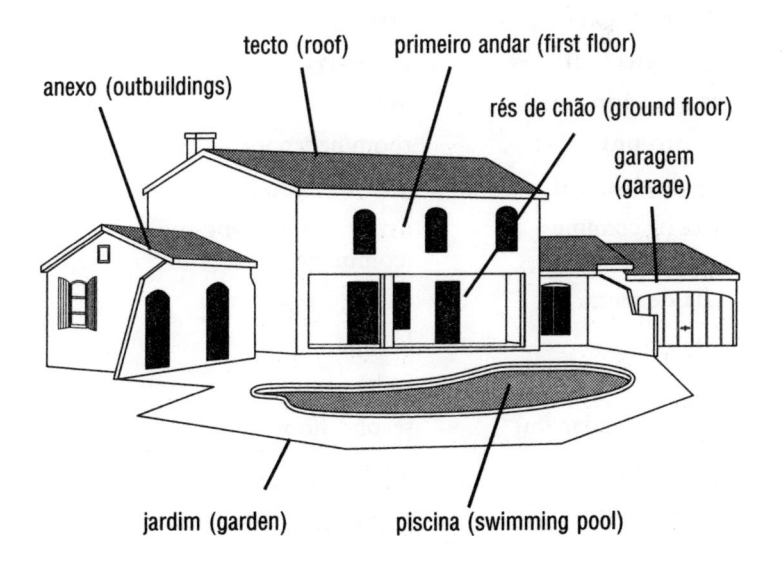

- tecto (roof)
- primeiro andar (first floor)
- anexo (outbuildings)
- rés de chão (ground floor)
- garagem (garage)
- jardim (garden)
- piscina (swimming pool)

abastecimento (m)	supply (water, electricity etc.)
anexo (m)	outbuilding
casa de banho (f)	bathroom
cave (f)	cellar
chão em parquet (m)	parquet floor
chão em pavimento (m)	tiled floor
comunal	communal
cozinha (f)	kitchen
despensa (f)	larder
quarto (m)	bedroom
escritório (m)	study
fossa séptica (f)	septic tank
garagem (f)	garage
despesas de condomínio	service charges
jardim (m)	garden
lareira (f)	fireplace
piscina (f)	swimming pool
porão (m)	basement
primeiro andar (m)	first floor
propriedade (f)	property
proprietário (m)	owner
quarto (m)	room/bedroom
rés de chão (m)	ground floor
sala (f) comum	living room/dining-room (combined)
sala de jantar (f)	dining room
salão (m)	lounge
sanita (f)	toilet
segundo andar (m)	second floor
sótão (m)	attic/loft
terraço (m)	terrace

terreno (m)	grounds
tecto (m)	roof
varanda (f)	balcony
WC (m)	toilet

> **What's included in the price?**
>
> If the property is furnished when you view it, ask very carefully about what will be included in the sale price. As in the UK, fixtures and fittings are generally deemed to be part of the sale, but there is no obligation to leave anything not explicitly mentioned in the contract.
>
> If there is anything in the house that you would like to be there when it becomes yours, tell the agent or the vendor, agree a price and get it written into the initial contract. Most vendors are open to reasonable offers.

Found it?

You've found a place that's perfect, or as near as perfect as you can get within your budget. What next? There are three key questions that need answering:

- Is it worth the asking price?
- Is it really within your budget?
- If you intend to adapt, improve or extend the house, will you be allowed to do it?

To get the answers, ask the experts.

O engenheiro – the surveyor

Having a survey conducted is not the norm in Portugal as it is in the UK, but to be on the safe side, you would be well advised to get a survey done on any property more than a few years old. We had a friend who was recently saddled with a €12,000 bill for shoring up the front of her flat when she discovered that that nice fresh plaster on the wall was just covering up the cracks...

Your *solicitador* (solicitor) will also check a number of other factors which may affect the cost of the property:

- The land owned with the property. Old houses, especially in villages, may have one or more non-adjacent gardens or other plots of land. The expert will check with the *conservatória do registo predial* (land registry).

- The planning status of the property and its land, as shown on its *parecer camarário* (report of planning status). This will tell you what use may be made of the land, i.e. whether you can build on it or extend any existing buildings. We will have another look at this in Chapter 3.

- Any rights of way or other encumbrances on the property.

Os orçamentos – estimates

If there are limited jobs to do on the house, e.g. a new roof, new bathroom, rewiring, etc. you can ask local tradesmen for an *orçamento* (estimate). You can rely on an *orçamento* to give you an accurate cost of the finished work – as long as you take it up within a few months, and don't redefine the job. If there is more complicated work to be done, approach an *arquitecto* (architect). As well as drawing up the plans, some Portuguese architects will also get estimates and oversee the building job. We will come back to the *arquitecto* and *orçamento* in Chapter 3 when we look at building work.

English – Portuguese quick reference

The search – a pesquisa

buy (verb)	comprar
estate agent	agente imobiliário (m)
for sale	vende-se/à venda
home	vivenda (f)
house	casa (f)/moradia (f)
land	terreno (m)
modern	moderno

needs renovating	necessita remodelação
new	novo
new search	nova pesquisa (f)
next	seguinte
previous	anterior
purchase	compra (m)
room	divisão (f)
sale	venda (f)
search (noun)	pesquisa (f)
search (verb)	pesquisar
solicitor	solicitador (m)

Types of houses – os tipos de vivenda

agricultural land	terreno rústico (m)
building plot	solar (m)/lote (m)
country house	moradia rústica (f)
detached house	casa individual (f)
facing the sea/mountains	com vista do mar/da serra
farmhouse	quinta (f)
flat	apartamento (m)/andar (m)
for renovation	a remodelar
good condition	bom estado (m)
good views	boas vistas (fpl)
house	casa (f)/moradia (f)
house/home	vivenda (f)
housing development	urbanização (f)/ empreendimento (m)
ideal investment property	óptimo para investimento
in the country	rústico (adj)
mill	moinho (m)
modern house	vila (m)
near the sea	perto do mar

old	antigo
refurbished	remodelado
ruin	ruina (f)
semi-detached house	casa geminada (f)
terraced house	casa em banda (f)
with/without electricity	con/sem luz

Rooms and facilities – as divisões e as características

air conditioning	ar condicionado (m)
attic/loft	sótão (m)
balcony	varanda (f)
basement	porão (m)
bathroom	casa de banho (m)
bedroom	quarto (m)
cellar	cave (f)
central heating	aquecimento central (m)
central vacuuming	aspiração central (f)
communal	comunal
dining room	sala de jantar (f)
fireplace	lareira (f)
floor (first/second)	(primeiro/segundo) andar (m)
garage	garagem (f)
garden	jardim (m)
ground floor	rés de chão (m)
grounds	terreno (m)
kitchen	cozinha (f)
lift	elevador (m)
living room	sala (f) comum
lounge	salão (m)
number of bedrooms	tipologia (T1, T2, etc.)
open-plan kitchen	cozinha americana (f)

outbuilding	anexo (m)
owner	proprietário (m)
parquet floor	chão em parquet (m)
property	propriedade (f)
refurbished	remodelado (adj)
roof	tecto (m)
room	divisão (f)
septic tank	fossa séptica (f)
service charges	despesas de condomínio (fpl)
stone floor	chão em pavimento (m)
storey	andar (m)
study	escritório (m)
supply (water, etc.)	abastecimento (m)
swimming pool	piscina (f)
terrace	terraço (m)
with views of...	com vista de...

02 a venda – the sale

Almost the same...

When you buy a house in England or Wales, nothing is certain until you exchange contracts, close to the end of the process. In Portugal you and the seller are both heavily committed to the terms of the sale at the very beginning. You cannot be gazumped in Portugal, neither buyer nor seller can renegotiate the price, nor can either of you back out without paying hefty compensation, unless there's a very good reason. A sale may only be cancelled if agreed conditions are not met or if a mortgage cannot be obtained. The whole process should take two to three months – about the same time as in the UK.

The people involved in the sales process are slightly different to the UK. You have an *solicitador* (solicitor), and their role is a cut-down version of the UK solicitor. They will act in your interests, advising on the legal status of the property, conducting searches and so on.

The sale itself is handled by a civil servant called a *notário*. Their job is to ensure that the transfer of ownership is done fairly and properly – which is, of course, in your interests. It is quite normal for both parties to use the same *notário* – there is no conflict involved, and there is less chance of communication problems and delays. If you want your own *notário*, that is perfectly acceptable, and won't make any difference to the fees.

Finally, you may also get a third party involved – there are companies which offer services of *assistência burocrática* (bureaucratic assistance) who will deal with Portuguese bureaucracy on your behalf! You may want them to help out with registering for taxes and other official matters – more on this on page 41.

There are some differences on mortgages too. The authorities in Portugal are more concerned than those in the UK that people should not over-extend themselves. Portuguese banks will lend you a smaller proportion of the value of the property, and take your outgoings as well as your income into account when calculating the maximum loan.

A propriedade e a lei – ownership and the law

Who will own your house? And what do you want to happen when the owner or one of the owners dies? Portuguese inheritance law is not as proscriptive as its French or Spanish equivalents – which set minimum shares that the spouse and children must inherit – but you should still make out a will in Portugal, as your UK will cannot cover your Portuguese house. Under UK law, any overseas assets must be disposed of according to the law of the land, and under Portuguese law, if there is no local will, your estate may be divided between your children and spouse.

Many properties in Portugal are owned through an offshore company. This was common practice when property sales were subject to a hefty transfer tax called SISA, which could cost you up to 26% of the purchase price. Portugal has been overhauling its tax regime in the last few years, and SISA has now been replaced with a less painful tax called IMT (*Imposto Municipal sobres as Transmissões* – Municipal Transfer Tax). See page 41 for more details on the IMT and other property taxes.

O imposto sobre as susessões e as doações – inheritance tax

Until recently the rules on inheritance tax were horribly complicated, with rates varying according to the value of the inheritance and how you were related to the beneficiary. Fortunately, inheritance is another area of taxation which has been much simplified. You may now leave your property to a spouse, child or parent without them incurring any inheritance tax. If you leave it to a third party, they will have to pay a fixed rate stamp duty (*imposto de selo*) of 10%.

A sociedade holding imobiliária – property holding company

You can buy a house through a 'holding' company (the Portuguese use the English word), which exists solely to own the property. The shareholders are usually members of the family or a group of friends who are buying a property together.

This way of owning property gives you more flexibility over inheritance or future ownership of the property. By simply changing the share ownership in the company, the property can change hands without having to go through the lengthy and relatively expensive legal process. You also avoid incurring inheritance and capital gains tax.

Having a company own the property does entail some additional costs – the company has to be set up, and will have to file annual accounts, for instance, for which you'll probably need an accountant. But where friends want to pool their resources to buy a property, it can be a good solution. The company provides an ongoing vehicle for sharing expenses – and income if the property is rented out – and simplifies future changes of ownership, should any party later want to drop out.

There is however a serious issue which you should consider very carefully before diving into a company ownership structure to avoid tax. The tax reforms of recent years have not all been to the advantage of foreign property owners, and there has been a clampdown on using company ownership to avoid tax. The new property transfer tax which replaces the old tax regime levies a 15% rate on purchases made through an offshore company – a much higher rate than if you buy as an individual.

The authorities can also presume that the company earns a rental income based on its *valor tributável* (a valuation of the property for tax purposes), and will tax you via the company for this presumed income. Finally, there is an annual tax called the *imposto municipal sobre imóveis* (municipal property tax), sometimes also known by its old name, the *contribuição autárquica*. This is usually between 0.2 and 0.8% for privately-owned properties, but which is charged at 5% on properties owned by an offshore company.

Since these two charges are both annual, the savings you may make by avoiding one-off taxes will in the long term be offset by the extra ongoing costs. Many long-term owners have decided they are better off having their properties transferred from company ownership back into their own names – even though this means they have to pay substantial capital gains and transfer taxes in the process.

> **Take expert advice**
>
> In all matters legal and financial, this book aims to give general guidance only. If you have any doubts or queries about what is right for you, talk to a properly qualified Portuguese specialist before making any decisions.

A compra duma propriedade nova – buying a new property

There are two main approaches to buying a new-build property. The most common way is to buy off-plan, in which you buy the house or apartment before or during building, on the basis of a plan. These usually involve a large initial payment, typically 40%, followed by stage payments until the house is completed, at which point it is officially yours.

The alternative is to have one contract which sells you the building plot and a separate contract to build the house. This gives you the security of owning the plot outright from the outset – you will hear horror stories of people paying 90% of the cost of the property and then waiting for years for completion, during which time they have no legal right to anything. If you own the plot and the building work goes horribly awry, you can always turf the developers off your land and get someone else in to finish the job.

If you can't arrange this (developers are understandably reluctant to sell on this two-contract basis, especially on *urbanizações*), then at least push for the stage payments to be linked to specific building milestones, and try to introduce penalty clauses for late completion.

A oferta de compra – the purchase offer

Having found a resale property that you like, agreed a price with the vendor, and decided on the form of ownership, it's time to start the buying process. At the first stage, the *agente* may ask you to sign an *oferta de compra* (offer to buy), and pay a good-faith deposit of around €1000. These are more common in commercial purchases than in domestic ones, and are more likely to be used if you have not yet agreed the price with the vendor. Essentially it states that you are willing to buy the property at a given price. If the vendor accepts the offer, this proposition will be used as the basis of the contract of sale.

O contrato de promessa de compra e venda – the sale contract

At this point a *contrato de promessa de compra e venda* (promissory contract of sale and purchase) will be drawn up. This document does not transfer the property, but commits both you and the seller to the sale and purchase. On signing the contract you will pay a *déposito* (deposit) of around 10%, and you will be legally bound to the sale. If you pull out now, you lose the deposit; similarly, if the seller pulls out you get double your deposit back.

This is quite scary for Brits, as we are used to being able to change our minds right up until the last minute – but if you've ever been messed about on a house sale (as many of us have), you will see the up-side to this arrangement!

Remember that we are still very early in the process, and you have not had surveys or searches carried out – which might bring up perfectly legitimate reasons for you to want to back out. You must make sure that the contract includes some *cláusulas de anulação* (annulling clauses) which allow you to pull out without losing your deposit. There are several standard clauses which cover situations such as the following:

- unsatisfactory results from surveys or searches
- lack of planning permission for expected building work
- your failure to secure a mortgage
- the seller's failure to clear existing debts on the property – in Portugal, mortgages are attached to a property, not to the person, and it is possible to inherit someone else's debt if you're not careful!

Be as specific as possible on your conditions – make it a specific mortgage at a specific rate, otherwise the seller can insist that you proceed with the sale on the grounds that there are other mortgages available, even if they're not good value for you. Your *solicitador* will help you draw up sufficient clauses to give you a reasonable way out if you need it.

The contract must also contain the following information:

- description of the property, its dimensions and related costs. Where appropriate, it should clearly identify the *zonas comuns* (communal areas) and *despesas de condomínio* (service charges).
- Details of the *notário* and the buying and selling parties.
- The price and date of payments. For stage payments on new-build properties, building milestones and penalties for late completion should also be specified if possible.
- The amount of the deposit
- If you will be taking out a *hipoteca* (mortgage), how much you are borrowing and where you hope to borrow from.
- A date for signing the deed of sale.

The property is now taken off the market. The deposit must be in Euros, and if you do not yet have a Portuguese bank account, you may not be able to make immediate payment. This should not be a problem. You can agree to pay within a set time, paying by bank transfer once you get back to the UK.

Between now and the signing of the *escritura* (deed of sale) which officially transfers ownership to you, your *solicitador* will conduct the necessary checks and searches, and you will need to arrange finances.

You will also need to pop down to the local *Finanças* (tax office) to get yourself an *NIF* – a *número de identificação fiscal* (fiscal ID number) and a *cartão de contribuinte* (taxpayer's card), which you will need for tax purposes.

It's a good idea to open a Portuguese bank account too, to make it easier to pay bills by *débito directo* (direct debit).

> ### Play fair, play safe
>
> Understating the value of your property on the *escritura* can seem like a 'nice little earner'. People often used to put a different price in the *escritura* to the amount which actually changed hands. The *escritura* is the basis for calculating taxes, so it pays to undervalue the property... but you do so at your own risk!
>
> As part of the ongoing tax reforms, properties in Portugal are being reassessed by the authorities on their *valor tributável* (notional value for tax purposes). If it turns out you have undervalued your house on the *escritura* you may be made to pay stiff penalties.

A documentação – the documentation

You should see copies of various documents from the seller before signing the contract, depending on whether the property is a new build or resale. In either case, you should ask to see any relevant building permits and guarantees covering structural work and safety issues such as electrical installations. If you are planning to build or extend the property, you should go to the *câmara* (town hall) and get a *parecer da câmara* (planning status report) and a *licença de utilização* (usage licence), which will set out any planning restrictions.

For new build properties:

* *licença de habitabilidade* or *cédula de habitação* – a certificate to say that the property is fit for habitation.

For resale properties:

* the vendor's *escritura* and *certidão de registo* (land registry record) to prove the seller's ownership and to establish whether there are any debts attached to the property.
* a *caderneta predial* (tax document) showing the property's *valor tributável*.
* recent bills for utilities and service charges.

Any outstanding debts on the property are supposed to be recorded on the *certidão de registo*, but in practice it can take a long time for debts to be logged there. The *certidão* is therefore no guarantee that there are not more recent debts attached to the property, and your lawyer should check with the *conservatória do registo predial* (land registry office) on the day of completion to ensure it is still in the clear.

> ### Can your Portuguese cope?
>
> You need good Portuguese to be able to cope with the legal and technical terminology in the contract and related documents yourself. If you have any doubts about your ability to fully understand the documents, ask for copies, take them away and get them translated. Take advice from an English-speaking *solicitador* or a UK solicitor who understands Portuguese property law.
>
> Don't sign anything lightly.

Lexicon: o contrato – the contract

assistência burocrática (f)	service to help you deal with bureaucracy
cédula de habitação (f)	certificate to prove house is habitable
certidão do registo (f)	land registry entry
cláusula penal (f)	penalty clause
cláusulas de anulação (fpl)	conditions to be met for the agreement to be valid
compra (f)	purchase
comprador (m)	purchaser (male)
compradora (f)	purchaser (female)
contrato de promessa de compra e venda (m)	contract of sale
escritura (f)	deed of sale
despesas de condomínio (f)	service charges
hipoteca (f)	mortgage
notário (m)	notary, lawyer and public official

oferta de compra (f)	offer to buy, at a stated price – this is not a contract
oferta de venda (f)	offer to sell at a stated price – again, this not a contract
parecer da câmara (m)	planning status report
sociedade holding imobiliária (f)	property holding company
solicitador (m)	solicitor
venda (f)	sale
vendedor (m)	seller (male)
vendedora (f)	seller (female)
zonas comuns (fpl)	communal areas

Finance

For the sale to be completed, the purchase money must be transferred. There are three main ways to do this:

- You can transfer the cash from your UK bank account, converted into Euros, using interbank transfer. You will need to know the relevant bank details, including the IBAN (International Bank Account Number) to do this. The money should take between three and five days to reach its destination, but can take longer. There is also a 'same day' transfer service – which can take three days or more to get through. Make the transfer in good time, and check that it arrives!

- Obtain from your UK bank a banker's draft in Euros and give this to the *notário*. A draft guarantees that the money exists and will be paid.

- Open a bank account in Portugal, transfer the necessary funds into it and write out a Portuguese cheque or draft. You will have to have a Portuguese bank account if you take out a Portuguese mortgage, but it will in any case make your continuing life there much simpler. With a Portuguese account you can set up direct debits to pay the tax and utility bills and save a lot of trouble – being out of the country at the time is not an acceptable excuse for not paying a bill when it is due! It takes minutes to open a Portuguese bank account.

You will need a passport, your *NIF* (ID for Portuguese tax purposes – see page 34) – and proof of your (intended) address in Portugal. They will happily arrange to send your correspondence to your UK address if required.

Mortgages

Portuguese mortgage lenders usually require a deposit of at least 25% of the purchase price, and may want up to 50% from foreign, non-resident borrowers. Interest rates are currently lower than in the UK, and are usually fixed. Repayment is the norm, there are very few lenders who offer interest-only mortgages. Don't count on rental income to pay your mortgage either – lenders will not generally take possible rental income into account when calculating how much they'll lend you. Buy-to-let deals are very uncommon, though some lenders may consider it in solid rental areas.

Portuguese banks are more cautious than those in the UK. You cannot normally borrow more than four times your total income. More to the point, you cannot normally borrow so much that your total debt ratio – outgoings, including other loan repayments compared to net income – is higher than 33%. If you have a high income or you are asking to borrow a small percentage of the property's value, then the bank may allow a higher ratio.

Do you have the cash?

The mortgage can only cover the property itself, not the legal costs of buying it (10-15%, see page 40), so you must have the cash for these too. For example, with a €100,000 house you would need at least €25,000 for the deposit and €15,000 for the fees and taxes. With all the other inevitable costs of moving and settling, you would be ill-advised to start out on the venture without at least €50,000 to hand.

If you take out a Portuguese mortgage, do bear in mind that interest rates can change and that exchange rates do vary. A 25-year €100,000 mortgage now costs around £4,000 p.a. An increase of 1% in the interest rate, would increase it by a little over £400. A fall in the exchange rate from €1.45 to the pound to €1.3 would cost about the same. Play safe and don't borrow too close to your limits!

If you have plenty of equity in your UK house, you could remortgage it to release funds for an outright purchase in Portugal. If you do this, you must organise the remortgage before signing the initial contract, or have a *cláusula de anulação* written into it to cover the possibility of the remortgage not going through. The sale cannot be cancelled without losing your deposit if a remortgage is not obtained.

Whatever you do, take good advice and compare costs.

A escritura – the deed of sale

This is the document that transfers ownership. In drawing it up, the *notário* will have checked the vendor's right to sell, the boundaries of the property and any rights of way or restrictions on it. You should ask to see a draft copy of the *escritura* some time before the transfer day. This will give you a chance to have it translated and checked, if necessary, by a competent professional, and to raise any queries you may have. You will get to keep a copy of the final *escritura* and related documents, which may be needed in future for legal purposes.

The original deeds are stored by the *notário*, but you must get a certified copy as soon as possible (preferably on the day of completion) and send it to the *conservatória do registo predial* to register your ownership of the property. Until the registration process is complete, it is still possible for the previous owner to lodge fraudulent charges against the property, for which you will become liable.

A procuração pública – power of attorney

If it is not convenient for you to go – perhaps at very short notice – to the *notário*'s office to sign the contract, you can give someone a power of attorney to sign for you. The document to set up the power of attorney must comply with Portuguese requirements, but is then signed before a notary public in the UK, to be authenticated. Some UK agents will suggest you give them power of attorney to save you the cost of another trip to Portugal – it's all above board, but only do it if you feel you can trust them.

Fees and charges

Notários perform a public function, and their fees are set by the state, on a sliding scale according to the value of the property. They are non-negotiable, and there's no point in trying to shop around for a cheaper alternative. Transfer tax, registration costs and other official charges are also paid via the *notário*, so the total bill can be significant.

The fees and charges depend partly on whether you are buying a new build or resale property.

New build

- 19% VAT (*IVA – Imposto sobre o Valor Acrescentado*). which should be included in the sale price.

Resale

- *IMT – Imposto Municipal sobre as Transmissões onerosas* (municipal property transfer tax) ranges from 0% for properties under €80,000 up to 8% for properties worth between €250,000 and €500,000. It is a flat 6.5% on building land, and 15% if you are buying through an offshore company.

Costs common to all purchases

- *Notários'* fees are fixed amounts which increase with the value of the property, and will be between about 1.25 and 1.5%.
- 0.75 to 1% land registry fees
- 1 to 2% lawyer's fees

Property taxes

There are three property taxes, not all of which may apply.

IMI – imposto Municipal sobre Imóveis (municipal property tax)

This is a local tax that is paid by the owner of the house in a single instalment every year. It is normal practice for the buyer to reimburse the seller for the tax for the remaining portion of the year. The IMI will come to between 0.2 to 0.8%, depending on various factors, including the age and location of the property.

Do note that this tax is based on the property's value (*valor tributável*). If you buy a ruin and restore it to its former glory and beyond, the *IMI* can go up accordingly.

Other local taxes

Municipal authorities will also charge various taxes to cover local services such as *lixo* (rubbish collection). These are usually collected via your water bill.

Capital gains tax

There is no special capital gains tax in Portugal as such. If and when you sell the property, 50% of any profit you make is treated as ordinary income, so you will pay income tax on it. Rates vary from 12% to a top rate of 40%. If you are resident in Portugal and you reinvest the money in another property, you may not have to pay any tax on the profit.

A assistência burocrática – the bureaucratic go-between

In Portugal there is a whole class of services which do not exist in the UK – *assistência burocrática* is a professional service which deals with bureaucracy on your behalf. This is mainly to service the needs of foreign residents, though the Portuguese themselves sometimes take advantage of the service too, simply because of the amount of time you can waste standing in queues or being shunted from pillar to post. If you deal with the grey machine yourself, you'll save yourself a bit of money – but will probably realise quite quickly why people do use *assistência burocrática*!

Lexicon: a venda – the sale

certidão do registo (m)	document showing ownership and debts of a property
conservatória (f) do registo predial	land registry
débito directo (m)	direct debit
escritura (f)	deed of sale

IMI – Imposto Municipal sobre Imóveis (m)	local property tax
IMT – Imposto Municipal sobre as Transmissões (m)	property transfer tax
IVA – Imposto sobre o Valor Acrescentado (m)	VAT
valor tributável (m)	valuation of property for tax purposes

> **Tax rates, interest rates, exchange rates**
>
> All tax, interest and exchange rates given in this book refer to those at the time of writing, late 2004, and may have changed by the time you read this.

Os serviços – services

Utilities in Portugal are all supplied by a mixture of private and state-owned companies. The services are mostly good in towns and *urbanizações*, and slightly more erratic in rural areas. Gas is fairly cheap, but water and electricity are not.

The utilities that are already connected to your house should be transferred to your name by the *solicitador* handling the sale. If they don't provide this service for you, contact the vendor and get the details of their contracts. It should be simple enough to have the contracts transferred to your name at the appropriate time. Getting connected to mains water, electricity, gas or telephone for the first time may be a bit more involved and take a little longer to achieve. If your property is on an *urbanização*, connection to services should be arranged for you, and the cost included in the sale – developers should not charge you extra for this.

Electricity is supplied on a wide range of tariffs, which depend primarily on how much power you need to have on tap. You need to choose the level of supply, from 3kW to 36kW (15 to 60 amps), to match your possible peak demands. You can run the normal range of lights, TV, washing machine and other electrical appliances on a 9kW (45amp) supply, increasing to 12 or

15kW if you are running high-demand appliances such as an electric oven or heating system. Connection costs vary depending on your location.

The electrical current is 220 volts, which runs UK appliances, but you will need buy adaptors – or change the plugs – to be able to use them in round-pin sockets. Buy Portuguese, it's easier! Bills are sent out every two months, and you can pay by *débito directo* to avoid disconnection for missed payments. Alternatively, if you give the supplier your address in the UK they will send your bills there.

Gas, supplied by Gás de Portugal, is only piped to houses in the capital, so you will quite probably use *garrafas de gás* (bottles of butane) for your gas heating and cooking needs. These are cheap, last a decent amount of time and are widely available at garages and elsewhere. You can also arrange a contract to get them delivered to your door, which is handy – they're very heavy!

Water is usually metered with a standing or minimum consumption charge, which you will be charged even if you don't actually use any water during the period. The costs per cubic metre are stepped into three price bands, rising steeply as you use more water. Low-level consumption is reasonably priced, but as your monthly quota rises, so the cost per unit rises, and you could find that your swimming pool is costing you a fortune to keep full, especially in the hot, dry South. Some *urbanizações* may offer unlimited water supply deals – you will usually pay for the privilege, but at least you know up front what your bills are going to look like.

Lexicon: os serviços – services

água (m)	water
câmara (f)	town hall
electricidade (f)	electricity
garrafa de gás (f)	bottle of butane
gás (m)	gas
lixo (m)	rubbish

English – Portuguese quick reference

The initial contract – o contrato de promessa de compra e venda

agreement to buy	oferta de comprar (f)
bureaucratic services	assistência burocrática (f)
certificate of fitness for habitation	cédula de habitação (f)
conditional clauses	cláusulas de anulação (fpl)
contract of sale	contrato (m) de promessa de compra e venda
lawyer	solicitador (m)
mortgage	hipoteca (f)
notary	notário (m)
penalty clause	cláusula penal (f)
planning status	parecer da câmara (m)
property holding company	sociedade holding imobiliária (f)
purchase	compra (f)
purchaser	comprador (m)/compradora (f)
seller	vendedor (m)/vendedora (f)
service charges	despesas de condomínio (fpl)

The sale – a venda

deed of transfer	escritura (f)
fiscal value of property	valor tributável (m)
land registry	conservatória do registo predial (f)
land registry record	certidão do registo (f)
property tax	IMI – Imposto Municipal sobre Imóveis (m)
property transfer tax	IMT – Imposto Municipal sobre as Transmissões (m)
VAT	IVA – Imposto sobre o Valor Acrescentado (m)

Services – os serviços

bottle of butane	garrafa de gás (f)
electricity	electricidade (f)
gas	gás (m)
rubbish	lixo (m)
telephone	telefone (m)
town hall	câmara (f)
water	água (f)

03 as obras – building work

Almost the same...

The Portuguese have planning permission and building regulations the same as we do in the UK, but the extent to which it restricts your options depends on where you are and what you want to do. Heavily developed southern Portugal is awash with lavish villas and condominium complexes, and recently we have seen ultra-modern developments using glass walls and high-tech energy-efficient materials. But you might find that if you wanted to turn your little stone cottage in a small rural village into a mini-Guggenheim, you may run into opposition from the local *câmara* (town hall).

Whatever work you are doing – from relatively minor works such as moving a partition wall to major building works, you will need a *licença de obras* (building permit). Only builders who hold an *alvará* (builder's licence) can obtain a *licença*, and if you are going to build a new house, extend an existing one outwards or upwards, add a garage, outbuilding or pool, you will need to employ an *arquitecto* (architect) to draw up proper plans to support your application.

As in the UK, all building work is subject to local and national planning regulations, and health and safety rules.

Check at the câmara (town hall)

The *câmara* is where the planning permits are issued. It can take a longer or shorter time to get permissions agreed, and there can be more or fewer nits picked in the process. This liaison will be done by your *arquitecto* for larger works, and you might also employ a *solicitador* even for smaller jobs. However, if you can get involved in the process to some degree and show that you want to be part of their community, it could make things go more smoothly. It's not always easy to get hold of the right people, but once you do it's amazing how much good will a few words of broken Portuguese can get you!

Building and planning regulations vary from place to place, so try to arrange to discuss your plans with someone at the *câmara*, or with a local architect or builder. They will be able to give you a clear idea of what kind of permission is required and what you will need to do to get it.

PDM – the town planning brief

Almost all municipalities have a PDM *(Plan Director Municipal)* – a map and a planning brief that determines what use can be made of the land. If you're buying a plot of land, make sure that it is not in a *reserva ecológica* (ecological reserve) or *reserva agrícola* (farmland). Wherever you are buying, it's as well to check that any future developments won't alter the character of the neighbourhood. The PDM is usually updated every few years, but will probably not change radically from one version to the next except in areas of very rapid expansion.

Ask at the *câmara* to see the PDM. They should be happy to show it to you.

A licença de obras – the building permit

The first step is to go to the *câmara* and check out the planning documents for your property. Documents like the *parecer da câmara* and the *caderneta predial urbano* will show you what planning restrictions there are on your property. If your plans don't fit with this, you will probably find it easier to change your plans than to change the permissions!

Assuming there's no theoretical obstacle in those documents, the next step in getting a *licença* is to pick up a form. The forms are quite complicated (now you start to see why people employ an *assistência burocrática!*), and must be accompanied by supporting documents:

- a map showing the land's boundaries and access roads;
- a description of the project and the materials to be used;
- for larger works, you will also need detailed architect's drawings and plans.

Any new buildings must conform to regulations such as the ratio of house to land area, the height and pitch of the roof, the position of windows in relation to neighbouring properties, and assorted other factors.

When completed, the work will have to be signed off by whoever is in charge of the project – you, the *arquitecto*, or the head contractor. You will probably also have to request a *cédula de utilização* (usage licence) for new buildings and extensions.

Consultation with the *câmara* will reveal any special requirements in your area, e.g. the minimum distance from the house to the boundary of your land (usually at least 1m), or restrictions on the type of construction or roofing material.

Other permits

If you are going to demolish any buildings or uproot trees to clear space, you may also need other specific permits – ask your *arquitecto* or at the *câmara*.

The local council's architect will go through the application and may come back with alterations and requests. These must be accepted and acted on. Do not assume anything about the state of the application if you still haven't heard anything several weeks later. The wheels of Portuguese bureaucracy can turn very slowly and you may need to chase the matter up from time to time. Don't give up and start work anyway though – if you find later that the permission was not granted, they can make you undo the work at your own cost.

When you start the work, you must display an *alvará* (a certificate confirming that you have a *licença* for the work) on a panel at the front of the site. This should give the basic information about the work, and the name of the architect or builder, as appropriate.

Once it's all finished, you will need to inform the *câmara* so that they can carry out a *vistoria* (inspection). This is to confirm that the work done conforms to the approved plans; you need this for the changes to be recorded legally.

As obras e os construtores – the building and builders

O arquitecto – the architect

A Portuguese architect often doubles as project manager for the building work too – they will draw up plans, deal with the paperwork, find tradesmen, get estimates and oversee the work for you. There is no real equivalent in the UK – the nearest is the project manager that you might find on larger sites, or the small master builder who will bring in other trades as they are needed.

A good *arquitecto* should be able to draw on a wide knowledge of materials and techniques to suggest solutions that you would never have thought of yourself. If you want to have the work done while you are in the UK, then employing an *arquitecto* is an obvious solution even for the simpler jobs. Even if you are there yourself, employing an *arquitecto* should ensure that the job is done better, and the extra expense – probably 5–10% of the cost of the project – may be well worth it in the long run.

Finding tradesmen

By Portuguese law, all building tradesmen have to carry full insurance to cover their work, and each job also has to have insurance. (If you are organising the work yourself, you will have to arrange this.) The tradesmen also must be registered and have an *alvará* to prove it.

The number of non-Portuguese property owners in Portugal means that there are organisations which exist purely to offer this kind of assistance. Try the AFPOP (Association for Foreign Residents and Visitors to Portugal) – they also arrange discounts for members with many firms including builders. Visit their website at **www.afpop.com**.

DIY at your own risk!

If you do the work yourself or have it done by someone for 'cash in hand', it will not be included in the official paperwork for the property, and you could have problems when you come to sell it.

The informal quality checks work as well in Portugal as in the UK (often better!) especially in the rural areas. Tradesmen prefer to work locally, and to rely more on word of mouth than advertising for their business, so reputation is important. Ask your neighbours or vendors if they can recommend people for the work. Your *agente* will also be able to put you in touch with local builders, but as with anywhere else – use your judgement. Your best interests may not be top of the list for someone who stands to make a commission from a particular builder.

Ask to see examples of their work and if possible, talk to past clients. Keep an eye out for the names of builders on the notices where building is in progress. And if all else fails, Portugal has *Páginas Amarelas* (Yellow Pages) just as we do.

O orçamento – the estimate

When you have found your tradesman ask for an *orçamento* (estimate). You should not have to pay for this; most will offer an *orçamento gratis* (free estimate).

The *orçamento* sets the price and the specifications, and will be the finished price for the job – unless you change the specifications later. But do be clear about what you are asking for. There have been cases of people getting a *orçamento* for a bathroom to find that it only included equipment and delivery. Make sure that *instalação* (installation) is included in the *orçamento,* and if in doubt, ask your *solicitador* to help draw up a contract!

Other trades

- *pedreiro* – bricklayer
- *rebocador* – plasterer
- *carpinteiro* – carpenter
- *telhador* – roofer, working with tiles, slates or similar
- *canalizador* – plumber
- *eletricista* – electrician

We will meet these and other tradesmen in the rest of the book.

Lexicon: as obras – building work

arquitecto (m)	architect
artesão (m)	tradesman
formulário (m)	form
licença de obras (f)	building permit
lote (m)	building plot
orçamento (m)	estimate

orçamento gratis (m)	free estimate
parecer da câmara (m)	planning report on a property
presidente da câmara (m)	mayor
trabalhador (m)	workman

English – Portuguese quick reference

architect	arquitecto (m)
building permit	licença de obra (f)
building site	lote (m)
estimate	orçamento (m)/estimativo (m)
form	formulário (m)/impresso (m)
mayor	presidente (m) da câmara
planning document	parecer camarário (m)
tradesman	artesão (m)
workman	trabalhador (m)

04

a estrutura –
the structure

Almost the same...

Outside of the major tourist areas along the southern coast, the Portuguese are quite keen on preserving the cultural history of the built environment. We have listed buildings and preservation areas in the UK, and so do they. But they go further. The Portuguese believe that, though the house may belong to you, its external appearance is a matter of common concern. If you plan to build a new house, or make changes to an existing one, and want yours to stand out from its neighbours, think again. You can have your individuality, but it must be within the limits of the regional look.

The ornate stonework and wrought-iron balconies of grand old apartments in cities like Lisbon and Coimbra will be protected, and you may not be allowed a slate roof in amongst the terracotta tiles of a southern village – or red tile in the north, where stone and slate are the norm. Some things you won't want to change anyway – the flat roofs of the Algarve were originally used for drying fruits on, but now are perfect for private sunbathing.

The majority of British house purchases in Portugal are in *urbanizações*. The appearance of these ranges from simple whitewashed apartments and terraced houses with shared facilities, to groups of extravagant villas with huge French windows looking out over private pools set about with arches and waterfalls.

On a purely practical level, Portugal is in an earthquake zone – they are not frequent, but the one in 1755 which destroyed most of Lisbon has left a lasting impression – and all modern houses are built to withstand earthquakes. In the south, where the risk is higher, buildings usually have a reinforced concrete frame, with concrete floor and roof joists.

Old Portuguese houses tend to have solid walls, while cavity walls are standard in new properties, as they are in the UK. New houses may also be built of hollow red bricks, which are large and light and go up very quickly. Breeze blocks are also quite common, and offer better insulation.

Check at the câmara

- If you are planning any structural change to the house, either external *or* internal, talk to the planning officer at the *câmara* at an early stage – see Chapter 3.

A estrutura – the structure

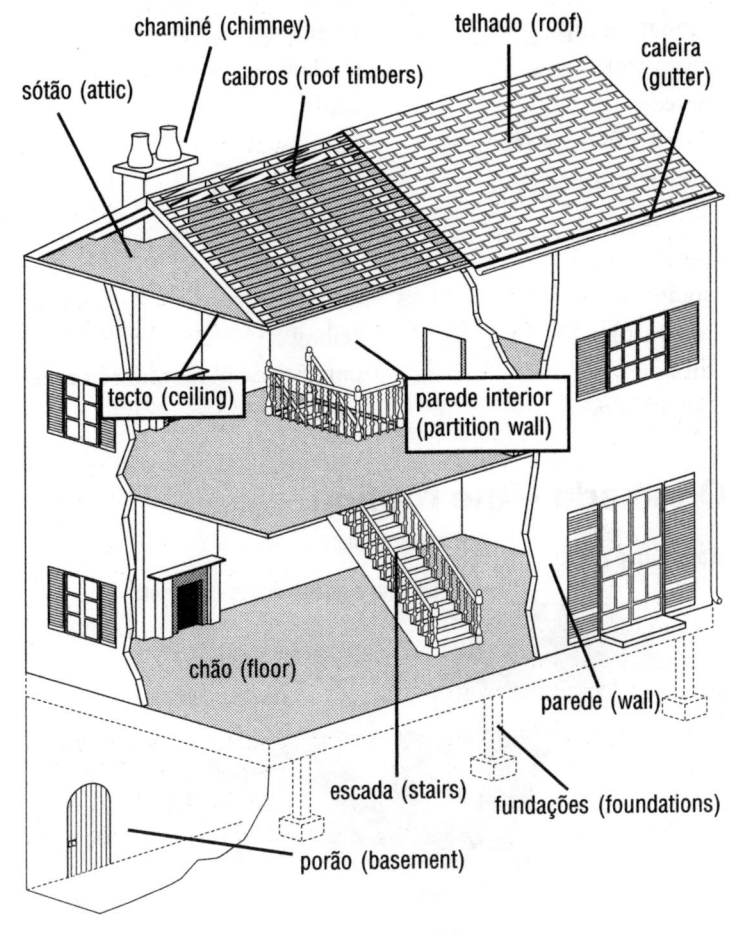

chaminé (chimney)
telhado (roof)
caleira (gutter)
caibros (roof timbers)
sótão (attic)
tecto (ceiling)
parede interior (partition wall)
chão (floor)
parede (wall)
escada (stairs)
fundações (foundations)
porão (basement)

bolor (m)	mould
caibros (mpl)	roof timbers
carcoma (f)	woodworm

chaminé (f)	chimney
chão (m)	floor
clarabóia (m)	light shaft
cobertura inclinada (m)	sloping roof
detritos (mpl)	rubbish
escada (f)	stairs
escombros (mpl)	rubble
fundações (fpl)	foundations
mofo (m)	mildew
parede (f)	wall
parede divisora (f)	party wall
parede interior (m)	partition wall
podridão (f)	rot
porão (m)	basement
sótão (m)	attic/loft
tecto (m)	ceiling
tabique (m)	partition wall (in older houses)
telhado (m)	roof

O telhado – the roofing

- espigão (hip ridge)
- cumeeira (ridge)
- telhado a quatro águas (hip roof)
- chaminé (chimney)
- revessa (valley)
- beiral (eaves)
- empena (gable end)

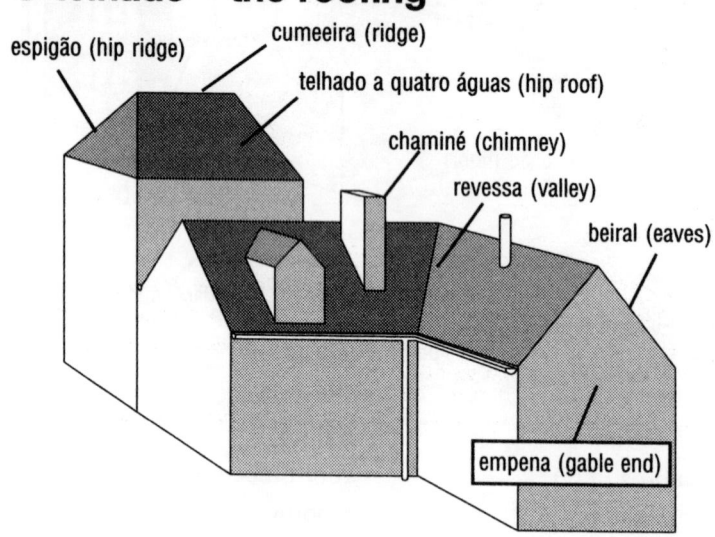

amarração (f)	roof truss
asna (f)	rafter
beiral (m)	eaves
caleira (f)	gutter
carvalho (m)	oak
chapa (f) de chumbo/de zinc	flashing – lead/zinc
clarabóia (f)	skylight
cumeeira (f)	ridge
empena (f)	gable end
espigão (f)	hip ridge
forro do beiral (m)	eaves board or fascia
frontão (m)	pediment (wall higher than the end of the roof)
papel-feltro betuminado (m)	lining felt
pendural (m)	vertical beam
pinho (m)	pine
revessa (f)	valley (inner angle where two roofs meet)
ripado (de telhado) (m)	lathing
telhado a quatro águas (m)	hip roof
terça (f)	purlin, horizontal tie on rafters
terraço (m)	terrace roof or balcony
trapeira (f)	window in roof
travessa (f)	horizontal beam
viga (f)	beam

Which word?

Sometimes there are several words for the same thing. Try to learn one of them well enough to be able to ask for it in a shop or when talking to a builder, and others well enough to recognise them when you hear them.

A cobertura – roofing materials

In southern Portugal, the risk of earthquakes means that all new houses are built from reinforced concrete – even the roof. Tiles are either laid directly on the concrete roof beams, or a solid concrete layer may be laid first. In older houses and elsewhere, the roof will normally be made from wooden rafters on a ridge beam and wall plates, braced by horizontal beams and lined with cane.

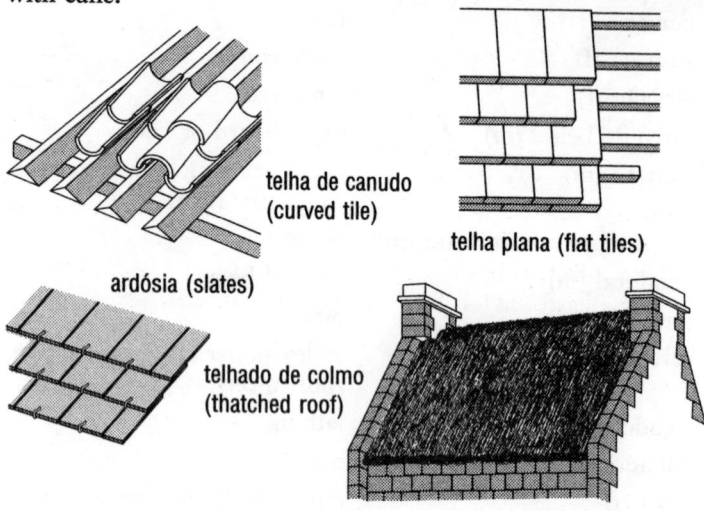

telha de canudo (curved tile)

telha plana (flat tiles)

ardósia (slates)

telhado de colmo (thatched roof)

As in the UK, you will not find lining felt under the tiles of older houses, unless they have been reroofed recently.

ardósia (f)	slate
barro vermelho (m)	clay
papel-feltro betuminado (m)	roofing felt
prego (m) de telhado de ardósia	slate clip
telha (f)	tile
telha de canudo (f)	curved tile
telha plana (f)	flat tile
telhado	roof...
... de colmo (m)	thatched roof
... de madeira (m)	wooden roof
... de papel betuminado (m)	bitumen roof

Roofing tradesmen

- If you want to build, adapt or mend the roofing timbers, you need *um carpinteiro* (a carpenter).
- If you need to replace or mend a roof, you need *um telhador* (a roofer).

As paredes – walls

Walls start from foundations, though not necessarily... In older houses, especially in country areas and where large stones were the building material, the walls were often built directly on the ground. Two possible problems can arise from this. You can get subsidence, though with an old house it's a reasonable bet that it has sunk as much as it's going to. You may also have rising damp, as there will be no barrier beneath the stones. The damp problem will be worse if the original – breathing – floor of beaten earth or flagstones has been replaced by concrete and tiles.

alicerce (m)	footing
alvenaria (f)	masonry/brickwork
cascalho (m)	hardcore
excavação (f)	excavation
fundações (fpl)	foundations
humidade (f)	damp
humidade nas paredes (f)	rising damp
isolamento da humidade (m)	damp course
parede (f)	wall
racha (f)	crack!
vala (f)	trench

External walls

For new building, the Portuguese use quite a lot of *tijolos furados* (hollow concrete or clay blocks). These come in a range of sizes and cross-sections, offering different weight to strength ratios. The resulting walls are not attractive when bare, but they are not intended to remain so. The outside is normally rendered with mortar and whitewashed. The inside is rendered or tiled.

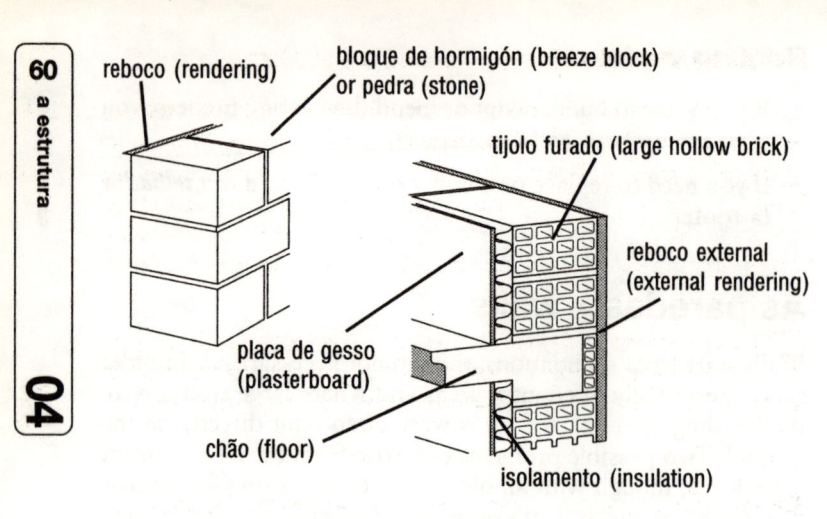

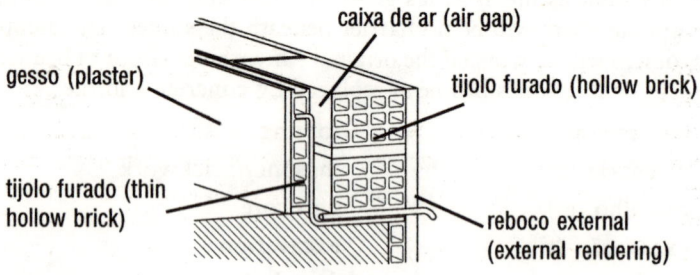

reboco (rendering)
bloque de hormigón (breeze block) or **pedra** (stone)
tijolo furado (large hollow brick)
reboco external (external rendering)
placa de gesso (plasterboard)
chão (floor)
isolamento (insulation)

caixa de ar (air gap)
gesso (plaster)
tijolo furado (hollow brick)
tijolo furado (thin hollow brick)
reboco external (external rendering)

Where a wall is built with a cavity, the structure is usually different from in the UK. Here a cavity wall has an inner load-bearing skin of brick or breeze block, and an outer skin of brick. In Portugal the cavity is formed by adding a thin inner skin to a standard thickness, load-bearing outer wall. Both inner and outer walls are often made of hollow bricks. In buildings with a concrete frame, neither the inner nor outer wall are load-bearing.

Instant walls!

If you want a very strong, solid wall quickly, build a dry wall – no mortar – of the hollowest bricks, slide reinforcing rods down through them, then fill with wet concrete.

As paredes interiores – partition walls

Some or all of the internal walls of a house will be *paredes interiores* – partitions. Smaller farms and terraced houses or apartments in towns are often built with the floor and ceiling joists supported solely by the outside walls. Keep this in mind when you look around old houses. *Paredes interiores* are easily removed and rebuilt elsewhere if you want to remodel the internal layout.

Old *paredes interiores* (also known as *tabiques*) are likely to be lathe and plaster or single-skin brick. New ones are quickly built from thin hollow bricks, plasterboard on wooden frames or plaster blocks.

Digression: blocos de gesso – plaster blocks

You won't find these in the UK, but plaster blocks are worth investigating as a quick and easy – if not very cheap – way of building internal walls. They are typically 66 × 50 cm, in widths from 7 to 12 cm and come in different weights and finishes – including waterproof ones for bathrooms and lightweight ones for loft conversions. They are assembled like brickwork – but much easier and faster – need no framework and can be cut with a wood saw. Exposed corners can be reinforced with an angled metal strip, if required. After a little fine filling of the ends and joints, the new wall is ready for decorating.

Wall materials

areia (f)	sand
arenita (f)	sandstone
argamassa (f)	mortar
betão (m)	concrete
betão armado (m)	reinforced concrete
bloco de cimento (m)	breeze block – either solid concrete with large moulded gaps, or cellular as in the UK
bloco de gesso (m)	plaster block
brita (f)	gravel
cal (f)	lime
caixa (f) de ar	air gap – may hold insulation

cimento (m)	cement
concreto (m)	concrete
de estrutura de madeira	half-timbered (of house)
gesso (m)	plaster
granito (m)	granite
grava pequena (f)	coarse sand
grés (m)	sandstone
isolamento (m)	insulation
mármore (m)	marble
placa de gesso (f)	plasterboard
pedra (f)	stone
pedra calcária (f)	limestone
pedra talhada (f)	dressed stone
perfil de ângulo (m)	angled strip for reinforcing corner of plaster wall
placa (f)	panel, plate
placa de gesso (f)	plasterboard
reboco (m)	internal wall lining – could be plasterboard
tábua (f)	board, panel
tijolo (m)	brick
tijolo furado (m)	hollow brick
tijolo refractário (m)	firebrick
verga (f)	lintel

Isolamento – insulation

cortiça granulada (f)	cork particles
esferovite (m)	polystyrene
fibra de vidro (f)	fibreglass
isopor (m)	polystyrene
janelas (fpl) de vidro duplo	double glazing
lã de rocha (f)	rockwool
poliuretano (m)	polyurethane
tábua isolante (f)	insulation panel
vermiculita (f)	mica particles

Building tradesmen

- A general building contractor is *um empreiteiro de construção*.
- If you want a bricklayer or stonemason, ask for *um pedreiro*.
- For plastering, you need *um rebocador*.

As ferramentas de constructor – builder's tools

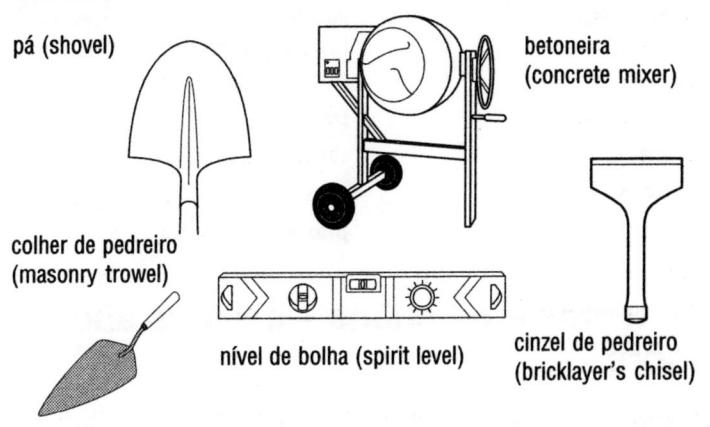

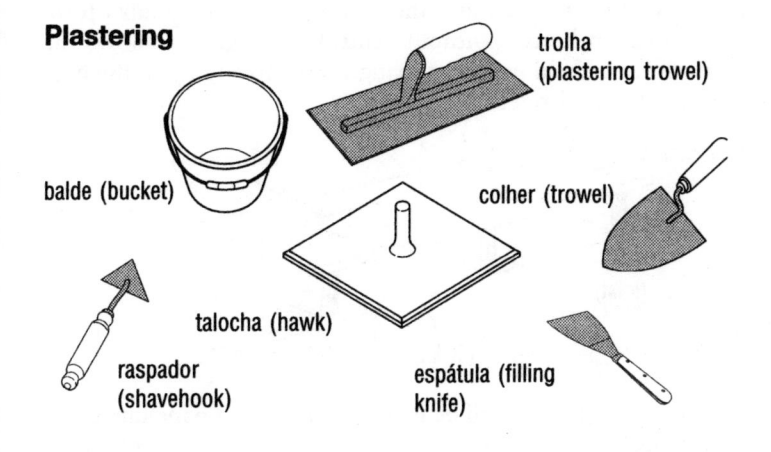

Brickwork

pá (shovel)

betoneira (concrete mixer)

colher de pedreiro (masonry trowel)

nível de bolha (spirit level)

cinzel de pedreiro (bricklayer's chisel)

Plastering

trolha (plastering trowel)

balde (bucket)

colher (trowel)

talocha (hawk)

raspador (shavehook)

espátula (filling knife)

balde (m)	bucket
betoneira (f)	concrete mixer
cinzel de pedreiro (m)	bricklayer's chisel
colher (f)	trowel
colher de pedreiro (f)	masonry trowel
espátula (f)	filling knife
nível de bolha (m)	spirit level
pá (f)	shovel
peneira (f)	riddle – box with a fine mesh base for removing lumps from sand or other dry material
picareta (f)	pick
raspador (m)	scraper, shavehook
talocha (f)	plastering float
trolha (f)	plastering trowel

Os tectos e os chãos – ceilings and floors

In many houses, the ceiling and floor are often – literally – two sides of the same thing! The traditional wooden floor consists of planks laid over joists, and the undersides of the planks form the ceiling. In houses without central heating, this allows the warmth from the downstairs living rooms to rise up to the bedrooms – but it also lets the noise up.

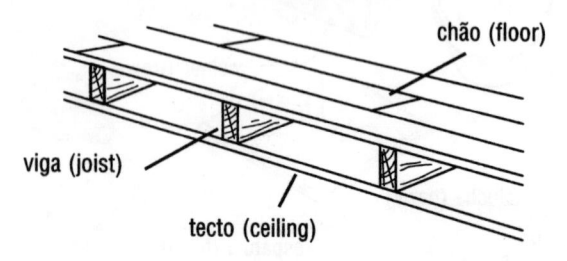

chão (floor)

viga (joist)

tecto (ceiling)

If there is a ceiling, it will be made of thin wood panelling or, as in the UK, of *ripado rebocado* (lathe and plaster) or *placas de gesso* (plasterboard).

In apartments and in more modern houses, the floor may be made of reinforced concrete with bricks in between. Apart from better sound-proofing, this also allows the use of ceramic or stone tiles for floors in upstairs rooms. Most apartment buildings (old and new) have stone tiled floors, which cannot be laid on a flexible wood base.

chão (m)	floor
lambris (m)	panelling (tongue and groove)
ripado rebocado (f)	lathe and plaster
tecto (m)	ceiling
viga (f)	joist

English – Portuguese quick reference

The structure – a estrutura

attic	sótão (m)
basement	porão (m)
ceiling	tecto (m)
chimney	chaminé (f)
floor	chão (m)
foundations	fundações (fpl)
mould	bolor (m)
party wall	parede divisora (f)
porch	pórtico (m)
roof	telhado (m)
rot	podrição (f)
rubbish	detritos (mpl)
stairs	escada (f)
wall	parede (f)
woodworm	carcoma (f)

Roofing – a cobertura

attic	sótão (m)
balcony	sacada (f)/veranda (f)

beam	viga (f)/travessa (f)
carpenter	carpinteiro (m)
ceiling	tecto (m)
clay	barro vermelho (m)
eaves	beiral (m)
flashing (lead/zinc)	chapa (f) (de chumbo/de zinc)
gable	empena (f)
hip ridge	espigão (m)
hip roof	telhado a quatro águas (m)
joiner	marceneiro (m)
lathe	ripado (m)
oak	carvalho (m)
pediment	frontão (m)
pine	pinho (m)
rafter	asna (f)
ridge	cumeeira (f)
roof	telhado (m)
roof timbers	caibros (mpl)
roof truss	amarração (f)/tesoura (f)
roofer	telhador (m)
roofing felt	papel-feltro betuminado (m)
skylight	clarabóia (f)
slate	ardósia (f)
slate clip	prego (m) de telhado de ardósia
sloping roof	cobertura inclinada (f)
terrace	terraço (m)
thatched roof	telhado de colmo (m)
tile	telha (f)
tile, curved (overtile)	telha de cobrir (f)
tile, curved (undertile)	telha canalha (f)
valley	revessa (f)

Walls – as paredes

air gap	caixa de ar (f)
breeze block	bloco de cimento (m)
brick	tijolo (m)
brick, hollow	tijolo furado (m)
bricklayer	pedreiro (m)
builder	empreiteiro (m) de construção
building (work)	construção (f)
carpenter	carpinteiro (m)
cement	cimento (m)
concrete	betão (m)
concrete, reinforced	betão armado (m)
crack (in wall)	racha (f)
damp	humidade (f)
damp course	isolante (m) da humidade
excavation	excavação (f)
floor	chão (m)
footing	alicerce (f)
foundations	fundações (fpl)
granite	granito (m)
half-timbered	de estrutura de madeira
insulation	isolamento (m)
joiner	marceneiro (m)
limestone	piedra calcária (f)
lining (for wall)	reboco (m)
lintel	verga (f)
marble	mármore (m)
mortar	argamassa (f)
panel	tábua (f)/placa (f)
partition wall	parede interior (f)
plaster	gesso (m)

plaster block	bloco (m) de gesso
plasterboard	placa (f) de gesso
plasterer	rebocador (m)
rendering	reboco external (m)
rising damp	humidade (f) nas paredes
rot	podrição (f)
rubbish	detritos (mpl)
rubble	escombros (mpl)
sand	areia (f)
sandstone	arenita (f)/grés (m)
stone	pedra (f)
stone, dressed	pedra talhada (f)
stonemason	pedreiro (m)
trench	vala (f)
wall	parede (f)

Tools – as ferramentas

bricklayer's chisel	cinzel de pedreiro (m)
bucket	balde (m)
concrete mixer	betoneira (f)
filling knife	espátula (f)
float	talocha (f)
pick	picarete (m)
plastering hawk	talocha (f)
plastering trowel	trolha (f)
riddle	peneira (m)
shavehook/scraper	raspador (m)
shovel/spade	pá (f)
spirit level	nível (m) de bolha
trowel	colher (f)

Ceilings and floors – os tectos e os chãos

ceiling	tecto (m)
floor	chão (m)
joist	viga (f)
lathe and plaster	ripado rebocado (m)
panelling	lambris (m)

05 a carpintaria – woodwork

Almost the same...

In the UK, building professionals make a distinction between joinery and carpentry, though for most of us it's all woodwork. In Portuguese you want *um carpinteiro* for any work in the house, whether the work is on structural timbers like floor joists or roof beams, or fitting staircases, windows, doors and the like. The other type of worker in wood is *un marceneiro* – a cabinet-maker.

The most obvious difference between the UK and Portugal is in the windows. Most Portuguese homes have shutters. We like shutters. They keep the sun out on a summer's day, the warmth in on a winter's night, the mosquitoes out when you're in bed and the burglars out when you're away. A side effect of shutters is that the windows must open inwards or slide sideways.

There's a small but significant difference in the way they hang doors – they use split hinges. We're fans of these too, and so will you be the next time that you are painting a door, laying floor tiles, moving big furniture or doing any other job where a door in a doorway is a nuisance. With split hinges, you just lift the door off and prop it up somewhere out of the way.

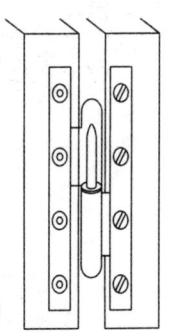

Split hinges make a simple job of hanging (and unhanging) doors – as long as you fit them the right way up!

Check at the câmara

* How you fit out a house internally is entirely up to you, but if you are adding or altering external doors or windows – especially on the publicly-visible sides of the house – check with the *câmara* if the new ones will be different from the others in the neighbourhood.

A carpintaria interna – internal woodwork

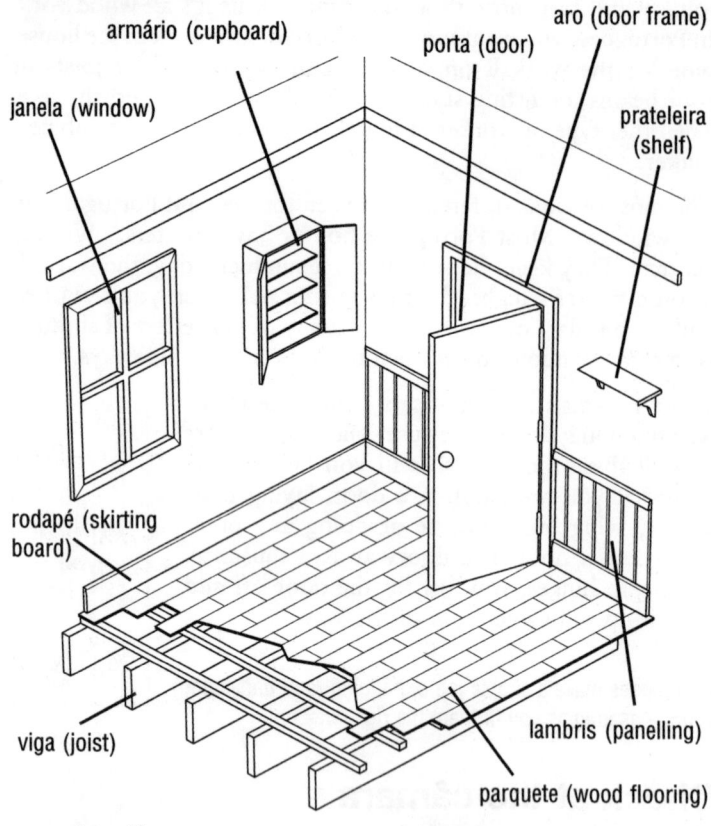

- armário (cupboard)
- aro (door frame)
- porta (door)
- janela (window)
- prateleira (shelf)
- rodapé (skirting board)
- viga (joist)
- lambris (panelling)
- parquete (wood flooring)

armário (f)	cupboard
armário embutido (m)	built-in cupboard
armário modulado (m)	wall unit
aro (m)	door frame
chão (m)	floor
janela (m)	window
lambris (m)	panelling
ombreira (f)	door or window jamb
parquete mosaico (m)	patterned wood flooring tiles
parquete tradicional (m)	parquet/wood block flooring

pavimento flutuante (m)	laminate flooring
porta (f)	door
prateleira (f)	shelf
rodapé (m)	skirting board
soalho de tábua corrida (m)	woodstrip flooring
tábua de soalho (f)	floorboard
tecto falso (m)	false ceiling
viga (f)	joist

Wood flooring

Wood flooring comes in several varieties:

- *parquete tradicional* – wooden parquet blocks (*tacos de madeira*) laid in a brick or herringbone pattern.

- *parquete mosaico* – small wooden tiles pre-arranged in mosaic patterns on a mesh backing, laid and glued to the floor like tiles.

- *tábua corrida* or *reguado* – long thin wooden strips, usually with a tongue and groove. Sometimes also used for wood-effect laminate flooring.

- *lamparquete* ('lam' as in 'laminate') – laminate flooring, supplied as tongue-and-groove panels. Also known as *pavimento flutuante* ('floating floor', so called because it is not actually nailed or stuck to the floor).

As portas – doors

aro (m)	frame
arquitrave (m)	architrave
bandeira (f)	fanlight
batente (m)	frame/door post
caixa (f) de correio	letter box
degrau (m)	doorstep
maçaneta (f)	door knob
massa de vidraceiro (f)	glazier's putty
moldura (f)	wooden beading for fixing glass

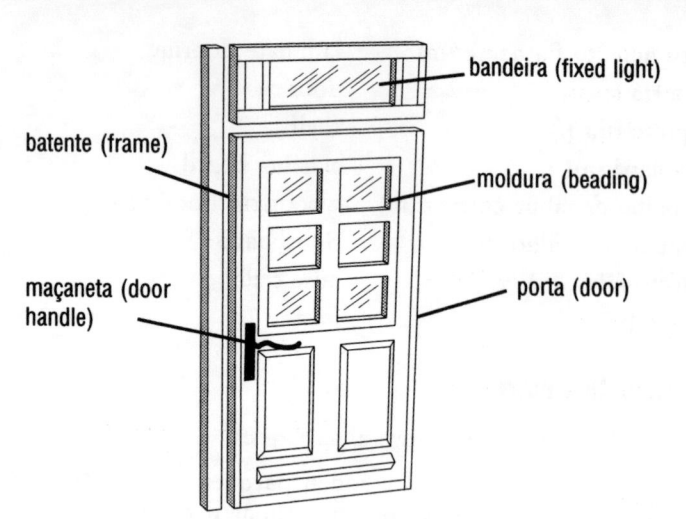

Labels on door diagram:
- bandeira (fixed light)
- batente (frame)
- moldura (beading)
- maçaneta (door handle)
- porta (door)

porta (f)	door
porta correr	sliding door
porta de segurança	high-security door
porta de vai-e-vem	swing door
puxador (m)	door knob
vidraça com caixilhos de chumbo (f)	leaded light

Ferragens para portas – hardware for doors

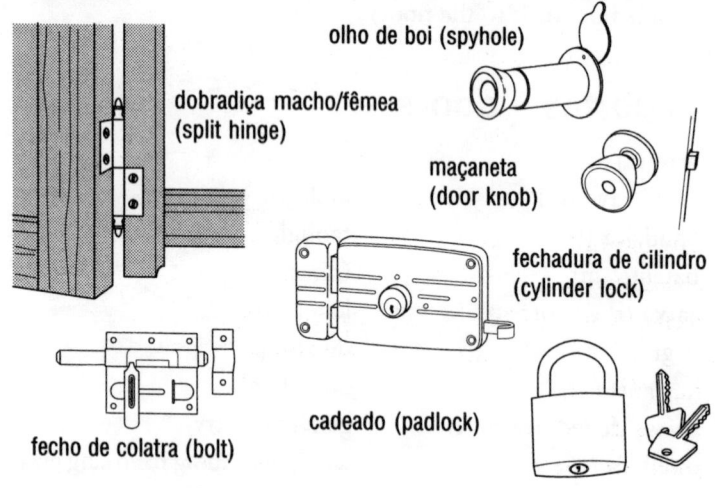

- olho de boi (spyhole)
- dobradiça macho/fêmea (split hinge)
- maçaneta (door knob)
- fechadura de cilindro (cylinder lock)
- fecho de colatra (bolt)
- cadeado (padlock)

buraco (m) da fechadura	keyhole
cadeado (m)	padlock
chave (f)	key
dobradiça (f)	hinge
dobradiça de braço	strap hinge for hanging heavy doors or shutters
dobradiça macho/fêmea	split hinge
fechadura (f)	lock
fechadura de cilindro	cylinder lock
fechadura para embutir	mortice lock
fecho (m)	catch or other means of keeping a door closed
fecho de colatra	bolt
maçaneta (f)	door knob
olho de boi (m)	spyhole for door

As janelas – windows

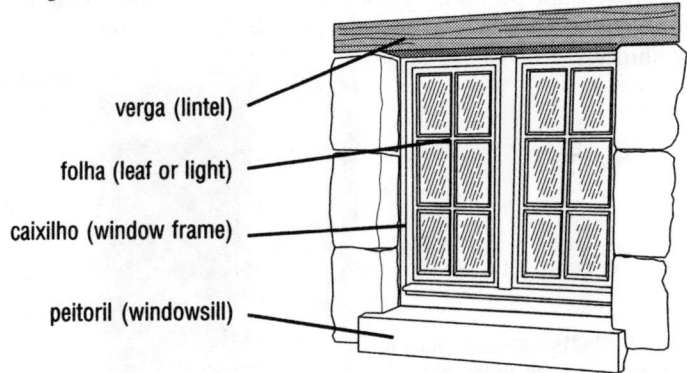

- verga (lintel)
- folha (leaf or light)
- caixilho (window frame)
- peitoril (windowsill)

caixilho (m)	window frame
clarabóia (f)	skylight
fecho (m)/trinco (m)	catch or other means of keeping a window closed
folha (f)	leaf or light
janela (f)	window
janela de correr	sliding window

janela de batente	casement window
janela de guilhotina	sash window
janela de mirador	oriel window
janela saliente	bay window
janelas de vidro duplo	double glazing
peitoril (m)	windowsill
porta-janela (f)	french window
verga (m)	lintel
vidraça (m)	pane
vidraceiro (m)	glazier
vidro (f)	glass
vidro duplo (m)	double-glazed pane

As persianas – shutters

Shutters are fitted on doors and windows to give extra security, shade and insulation. Strictly speaking, the word for 'shutter' is *portada*, while *persiana* refers to the kind of shutters with horizontal slats. In practice, however, *persiana* is used for any kind of shutter.

Wooden shutters are still found in the north, and can really enhance the appearance of a house.

There are many styles – in wood and other materials – but these days the most common are slatted shutters in aluminium or UPVC, which open outwards or roll up into a housing above the window. Those shutters which open flat against the outside wall are secured when closed, using a rod that holds the two leaves together and locks into the top and bottom of the frame.

Slatted shutters are more common in the south of Portugal. They provide ventilation and shade rather than insulation and shade.

Persiana dobrável

These may also be slatted, but open differently – they may fold concertina-style against the sides of the window frame, or slide away to either side of the window.

Persiana enrolável

These PVC or metal shutters are very common in more modern buildings. Roller shutters can be fitted inside the door or window frame, or project out from it. They can be hand-wound or electrically operated.

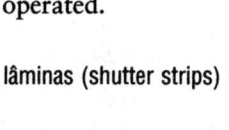

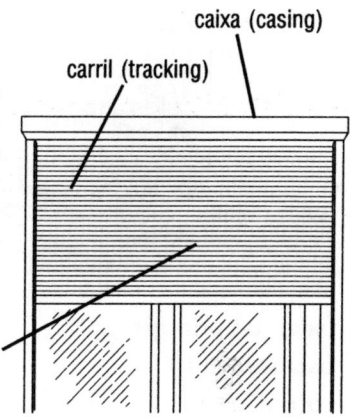

caixa (casing)
carril (tracking)
lâminas (shutter strips)

As persianas

caixa (f) para porta enrolável	casing for roller door
… para persiana enrolável	for roller shutter
carril (m)	tracking on roller shutters
dobradiça (f)	hinge
fecho (m)	latch
folha (f)	leaf, single shutter
guía (m)	tracking on roller shutters
lâminas (fpl)	shutter strips
persiana (f)	slatted shutter
persiana enrolável (f)	roller shutters

| portada (de madeira) (f) | wooden shutter |
| fecho (m) / trinco (m) | latch |

A escada – staircase

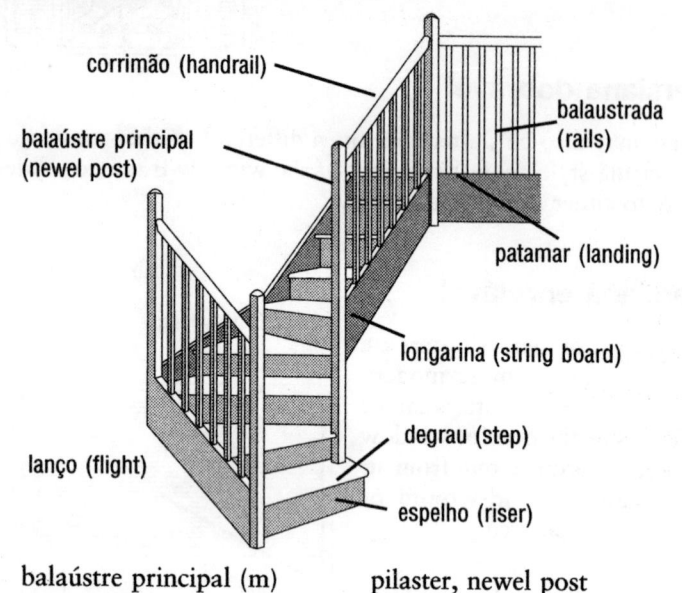

corrimão (handrail)
balaústre principal (newel post)
balaustrada (rails)
patamar (landing)
longarina (string board)
degrau (step)
lanço (flight)
espelho (riser)

balaústre principal (m)	pilaster, newel post
balaustrada (f)	rails
corrimão (m)	handrail
degrau (m)	step
escada (f)	staircase
escada portátil	ladder
escada dobrável (de sótão)	fold-away stairs, e.g. for loft
escada em espiral	spiral staircase
escadote (m) portátil	step ladder
espelho (m)	riser
lanço (m)	flight
longarina (f)	string board
patamar (m)	landing

Os armários e as prateleiras – cupboards and shelves

For most of us, making built-in cupboards and shelves isn't a *marcenaria* job – we just head for the nearest IKEA and buy flat-packs and shelving systems. In Portugal you'll find local DIY stores which stock furniture, such as Mestre Maco and Maxmat.

armário de alcove (m)	alcove cupboard
armário de canto (m)	corner cupboard
armário embutido (m)	fitted wardrobe/cupboard
chaveiro (m)	key hook
corbateiro (m)	tie rack
estante (f)	set of shelves
gaveta (f)	drawer
guarda-roupa (m)	wardrobe
porta-cabide (f)	clothes rail
portas (fpl) de correr	sliding doors
portas dobráveis	folding doors
porta-sapatos (m)	shoe rack
prateleira (f)	shelf

A madeira – wood

The wood section of a Portuguese *loja de bricolagem* looks much the same as one in any UK DIY store. Various shapes and sizes of a variety of woods are available *aplainado* (planed) or *cru* (unplaned).

aglomerado (m)	chipboard
carvalho (m)	oak
castanho (m)	chestnut
contraplacado (m)	plywood
contraplacado folheado (m)	plywood with wood veneer
de encaixe macho/fêmea	tongue and grooved
faia (f)	beech
folheado (m)	veneer

laminada (adj)	melamine-coated
madeira exótica (f)	tropical hardwood
MDF	MDF
mogno (m)	literally mahogany, but often refers to a dark wood finish for doors and furniture
moldura (f)	wooden beading
painel de aglomerado folheado	veneered chipboard panel
painel (m) de madeira	wood panel
pinho (m)	pine
platex (m)	hardboard

As ferramentas – tools

If you are going to do any *bricolagem* or *faça-você-mesmo* (do it yourself), you will need *umas ferramentas* (tools) and *uma caixa de ferramentas* (toolbox) – or even *uma oficina de bricolagem* (DIY workshop) – to keep them in. Here's an assortment of tools that you may find useful.

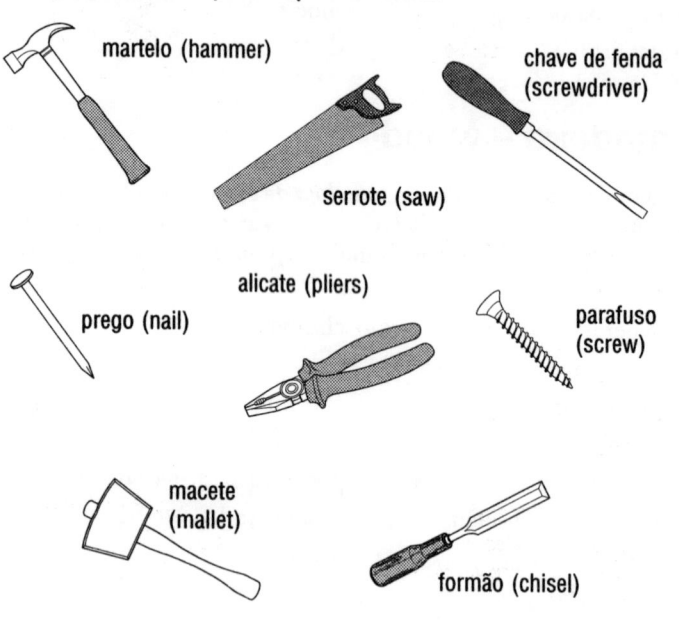

martelo (hammer)

chave de fenda (screwdriver)

serrote (saw)

prego (nail)

alicate (pliers)

parafuso (screw)

macete (mallet)

formão (chisel)

81 woodwork 05

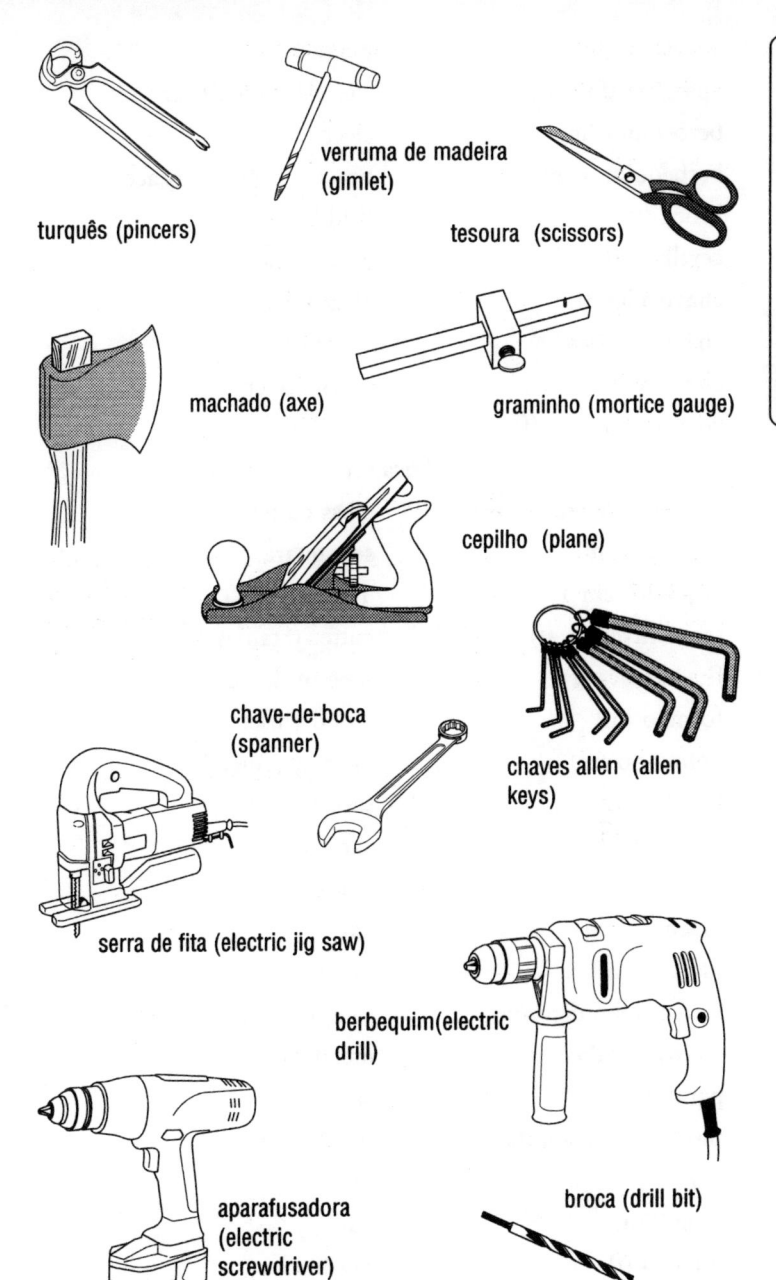

turquês (pincers)

verruma de madeira (gimlet)

tesoura (scissors)

machado (axe)

graminho (mortice gauge)

cepilho (plane)

chave-de-boca (spanner)

chaves allen (allen keys)

serra de fita (electric jig saw)

berbequim (electric drill)

aparafusadora (electric screwdriver)

broca (drill bit)

alicate (m)	pliers
aparafusadora (f)	electric screwdriver
berbequim (m)	electric drill
berbequim manual (m)	brace, of bit and brace
broca (f)	drill bit
cepilho (m)	plane
chave allen (f)	allen key
chave-de-boca (f)	spanner
chave de fenda (f)	screwdriver
cola de madeira (f)	wood glue
conjunto (m) de chaves-de-boca	set of spanners
cortador de vidro (m)	glass cutter
esquadro (m)	set square
esquadro em T (m)	T-square
faca universal (f)	cutter (Stanley knife)
fita métrica (f)	tape measure
formão (m)	wood chisel
graminho (m)	mortice gauge
lixa (f)	sandpaper
lixadeira (m)	sander
maço (m)	mallet
machado (m)	axe
martelo (m)	hammer
metro dobradiço (m)	folding rule
metro metálico (m)	metal rule
parafuso (m)	screw
pistola (f) de agrafar	staple gun
plaina (f)	plane
prego (m)	nail
punção (f)	bradawl
sem cabo	cordless

serra circular (f)	circular saw
serra (f) de recortes	jig saw
serrote (m)	saw
suta (f)	bevel square
tesoura (f)	scissors
turquês (m)	pincers
trado (m)	gimlet

> **How many?!**
>
> For several words where we use plurals, the Portuguese use singular, e.g. a pair of scissors is *uma tesoura* and a pair of pliers is *um alicate*. So, when you are buying tools in the *loja de bricolagem* (DIY store), try to remember to ask for *um alicate* not *uns alicates* – unless you have conscripted friends into helping out and need more than one pair!

English – Portuguese quick reference

Internal woodwork – a carpintaria interna

cupboard	armário (m)
false ceiling	tecto falso (m)
floor	chão (m)
floorboard	tábua (f) de soalho
frame, door	aro (m) or armação (m)
frame, window	caixilho (m)
joist	viga (f)
laminate flooring	lamparquete (m) or pavimento (m) flutuante
panelling	lambris (m)
shelf/set of shelves	prateleira (f)
skirting board	rodapé (m)
wardrobe	guarda-roupa (m)

wood flooring — parquete (m)/soalho (m) de tábua corrida

Doors – as portas

architrave	arquitrave (m)
beading for glass	moldura (f)
door	porta (f)
door frame	aro (m) or armação (m)
door jamb	ombreira (f)
door knob	maçaneta (m)
doorstep	degrau (m)
fanlight	bandeira (f)
letter box	caixa (f) de correio
sliding door	porta (f) correr
swing door	porta (f) de vai-e-vem

Hardware for doors – ferragens para portas

bolt	fecho (m) de colatra
catch	fecho (m)
cylinder lock	fechadura (f) de cilindro
door handle	maçaneta (f)
hinge	dobradiça (f)
hinge, split	dobradiça (f) macho/fêmea
key	chave (f)
keyhole	buraco (m) de fechadura
mortice lock	fechadura (f) para embutir
spyhole for door	olho de boi (m)

Windows – as janelas

bay window	janela saliente (f)
casement window	janela (f) de batentes
double glazing	janelas (fpl) de vidro duplo
French window	porta-janela (f)

glass	vidro (f)
leaf or light	folha (m)
lintel	verga (m)
pane	vidraça (f)
sash window	janela (f) de guilhotina
skylight	clarabóia (f)
window frame	caixilho (m)
window jamb	ombreira (f)
window pane	vidraça (f)
windowsill	peitoral (m)

Shutters – as persianas

hinge	dobradiça (f)
latch	fecho (m)/trinco (m)
roller shutter	persiana enrolável (f)
shutter, slatted	persiana (f)
shutter, wooden	portada (f) de madeira

Staircases – as escadas

flight of steps	lanço (m)
fold-away stairs	escada (f) dobrável (de sótão)
handrail	corrimão (m)
ladder	escada portátil (f)
landing	patamar (m)
newel post	balaústre principal (f)
rails	balaustrada (f)
riser	espelho (m)
spiral staircase	escada (f) em espiral
staircase	escada (f)
step	degrau (m)
step ladder	escadote portátil (m)

Cupboards and shelves – os armários e as prateleiras

clothes rail	porta-cabide (m)
cupboard	armário (m)
doors, folding	portas dobráveis (fpl)
doors, sliding	portas (fpl) de correr
drawer	gaveta (f)
fitted wardrobe	guarda-roupa embutido (m)
key hook	chaveiro (m)
shelf/set of shelves	prateleira (f)
shoe rack	porta-sapatos (m)
tie rack	corbateiro (m)
wardrobe	guarda-roupa (m)

Wood – a madeira

beading	moldura (f)
beech	faia (f)
chestnut	castanho (m)
chipboard	aglomerado (m)
hardboard	tábua dura (f) or platex (m)
melamine panel	tábua laminada (f)
oak	carvalho (m)
pine	pinho (m)
veneer	folheado (m)
plywood	contraplacado (m)
tongue and grooved panelling	de encaixe macho/fêmea lambris (m)
veneered plywood panel	contraplacado folheado (m)
veneered chipboard panel	painel de aglomerado folheado (m)
wood panel	tábua de madeira (f)

Tools – as ferramentas

allen key	chave (f) allen
axe	machado (f)
bevel square	suta (f)
brace, of bit and brace	berbequim manual (m)
chisel	formão (m)
cutter (Stanley knife)	faca universal (f)
drill bit	broca (f)
electric drill	berbequim (m)
electric screwdriver	aparafusadora (f)
folding rule	metro dobradiço (m)
gimlet	verruma (f) de madeira
glass cutter	cortador (m) de vidros
hammer	martelo (m)
jig saw	serra (f) de recortes
mallet	maço (m)
metal rule	metro metálico (m)
nail	prego (m)
pincers	turquês (m)
plane	cepilho (m) / plaina (f)
pliers	alicate (m)
rasp	grosa (f)
sander	lixadeira (f)
sandpaper	lixa (m)
saw	serrote (m)
saw, circular	serra circular (f)
scissors	tesoura (f)
screw	parafuso (m)
screwdriver	chave (f) de fenda
set square	esquadro (m)
spanner	chave-de-boca (f)

spanner, adjustable	chave-de-boca ajustável (f)
spanners, set of	conjunto (m) de chaves-de-boca
staple gun	pistola (f) de agrafar
tape measure	fita métrica (f)
T-square	esquadro em T (m)
wood glue	cola de madeira (f)

06
a canalização – plumbing

Almost the same...

Generally plumbing systems look much the same in Portugal and the UK, and as here the pipes and fittings come in both metric and imperial sizes. They are most commonly imperial, so if you're lucky, those lovely taps that you saw in Habitat might well fit on your bath in Portugal. Do check first though!

There are a few visible differences – bathrooms are usually fully tiled, and they tend to use more PVC pipes. The important differences, as you'd expect, are not so visible. The first point you need to note is that Portuguese houses have a direct water supply system – there's no cold tank. That'll give you a bit more space in the attic if you have one, but the important things in plumbing terms are that your water supply is at mains pressure, and that this may be higher than you get in the UK. In the UK, mains pressure is typically 0.5 bar or less and at most 1 bar. In Portugal, you may find pressure of 3 bars or higher. If the pressure is too high in your area, you can fit a *reductor de pressão* (regulator) to reduce it to a more reasonable level. You should definitely fit one if the pressure is above 3 bar, as many appliances are designed with that as a normal upper limit.

Water supply is managed locally in Portugal, by the municipal authorities or in some cases by private companies. Usage is metered, but there's usually a minimum consumption specified which you pay for regardless of whether you used that much or not (*consumo mínimo*) – effectively a standing charge.

Water shortages are not uncommon in the sunny South during dry periods, and you may find your supply rationed, sometimes quite severely, unless you have a private supply. Many new community developments do have a reliable private supply, but you will pay more for the privilege.

Water-saving tip

One way of reducing your water usage is to install taps with *aireadores*, which mix air in with the water to reduce the flow – they are much the same price as normal taps.

Check at the câmara

* If you are in a rural area and need to install *uma fossa séptica* (septic tank) you must get your plans approved at the *câmara* – see page 100.

A canalização – pipework

With modern materials and fixings, plumbing can be a job for the brave enthusiast – but even if you are not doing the plumbing yourself, it is helpful to know what the professionals are on about, and what you are paying for.

O abastecimento – supply

The water supply pipework is normally *hidronil*, a type of PVC piping which can be connected via threaded brass connectors and fittings. On copper pipes, the connections may be *soldado* (soldered) or *a rosca* (threaded, i.e. compression).

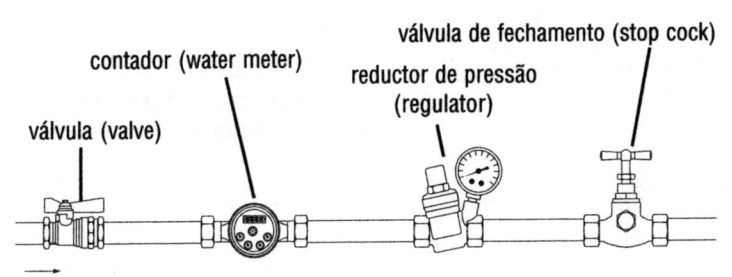

válvula de fechamento (stop cock)
contador (water meter)
reductor de pressão (regulator)
válvula (valve)

mains supply

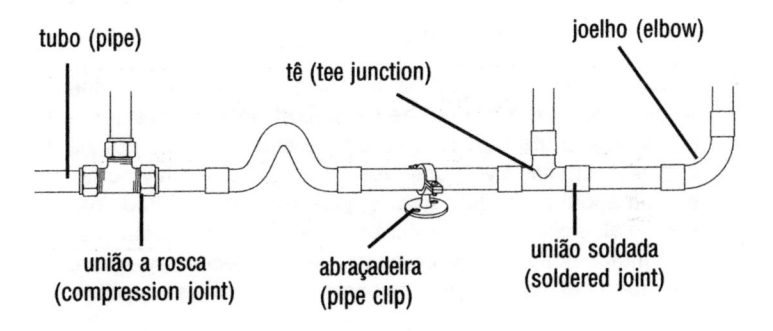

tubo (pipe)
joelho (elbow)
tê (tee junction)
união a rosca (compression joint)
abraçadeira (pipe clip)
união soldada (soldered joint)

abraçadeira (f)	pipe clip
água (f) da rede	mains water
bicha (f)	pipe, length of piping
chumbo (m)	lead
cobre (m)	copper
cobre recozido (m)	flexible copper, sold in rolls
contador (m) de água	water meter
joelho (m)	elbow/corner joint
luva (f)	sleeve
plástico (m)	plastic
PVC	PVC
reductor (m) de pressão	regulator – only needed where high pressure is a problem
tê (m)	tee junction
torneira (f)	tap
torneira (f) com aireador	aerator tap
tubo (m)	pipe
tubos flexíveis (m)	flexible pipes, often used to connect sink and bath taps to the fixed pipes
união (f)	joint
união de redução (f)	reducing joint
válvula (f)	valve, sluice gate
válvula de descarga	drain cock
válvula de fechamento	stop cock

The meter never lies

In some older apartment blocks there is one meter for the whole block, with the bill being shared between residents according to the size of their apartment. This may not be very economical if you only use the flat as a holiday home, so you should look into getting your own meter fitted. You should also check your water bills carefully, and install your own meter alongside the company meter if necessary – there are reports of overcharging by some unscrupulous suppliers.

Os tubos de esgoto – waste water system

There are two systems: *as caleiras* (guttering) for *as águas pluviais* (rain water) and the internal system for *as águas residuais* (waste water from sinks, baths, and toilets).

Guttering can be installed by a builder or *telhador* (roofer). Galvanised, i.e. zinc-coated, iron was commonly used for guttering, but most is now PVC.

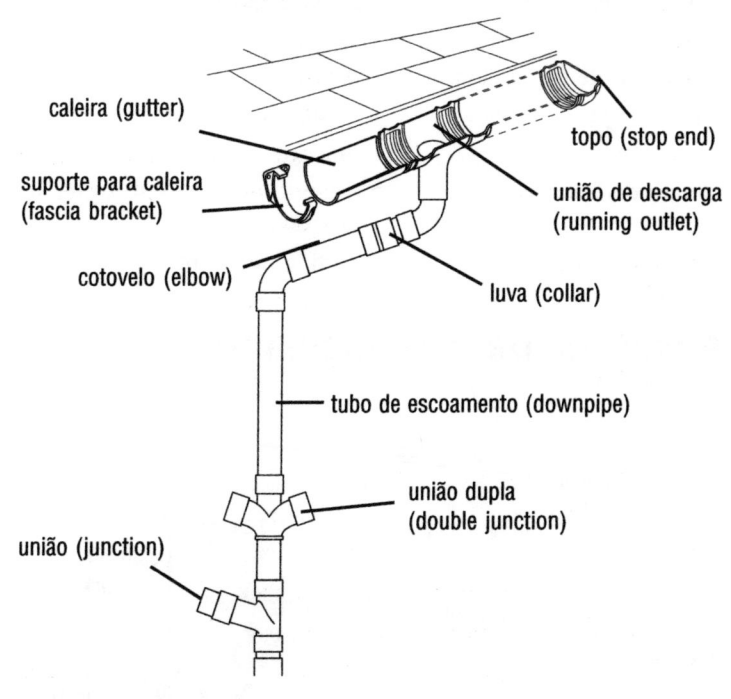

- caleira (gutter)
- suporte para caleira (fascia bracket)
- cotovelo (elbow)
- topo (stop end)
- união de descarga (running outlet)
- luva (collar)
- tubo de escoamento (downpipe)
- união dupla (double junction)
- união (junction)

For the internal systems, carrying *as águas residuais*, you need *um canalizador* (plumber).

Many rural areas are still not connected to mains sewerage – sewage treatment plants are surprisingly rare away from major towns and cities. *Fossas sépticas* (septic tanks) are common, and dumping into cesspools or the sea still happens, though it is becoming less frequent. If you are installing a waste water system you should consult the *câmara* to find out whether there is a mains drain to connect to, and if not, what your options are.

águas pluviais (fpl)	rain water
águas residuais (fpl)	domestic waste water
caleira (f)	gutter
ferro fundido (m)	cast iron
fondo (m)	stop end for gutter
ladrão (m)	overflow
luva (f)	collar, coupler
suporte (m) para caleira	fascia bracket
topo (m)	stop end for gutter
tubo (m) de escoamento	downpipe
tubos (mpl) de esgoto	waste pipes
união (f)	junction
união de descarga (f)	running outlet, joins gutter to downpipe
união dupla (f)	double junction

A casa de banho – the bathroom

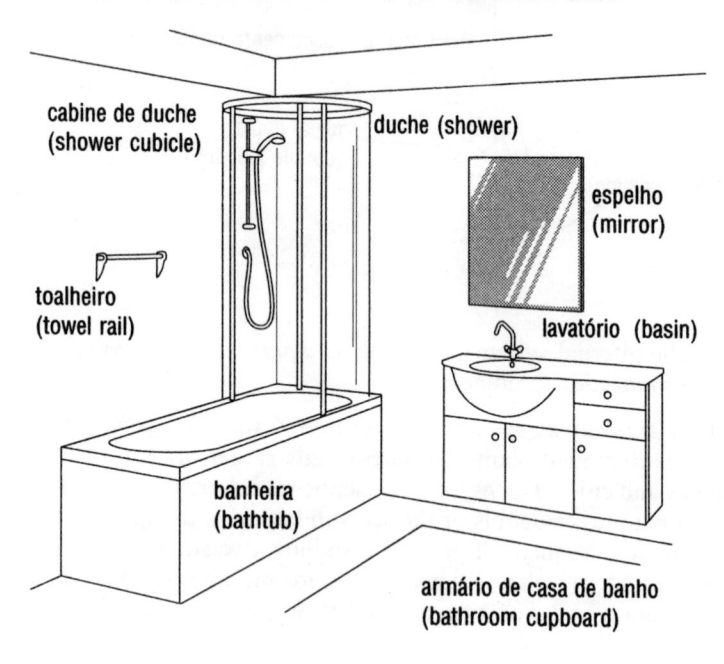

- cabine de duche (shower cubicle)
- duche (shower)
- espelho (mirror)
- toalheiro (towel rail)
- lavatório (basin)
- banheira (bathtub)
- armário de casa de banho (bathroom cupboard)

If you want a typical Portuguese bathroom, you need lots of tiles – ceramic tiles on the floor and right up the walls. Tiles mean lower maintenance and easier cleaning, and cold-to-stand-on-after-a-hot-bath is not the same problem in the warmer climate. Bidets are not a universal fixture, though some Portuguese brought up on them may still find the idea of not having a bidet somehow primitive and unhygienic.

As an alternative to an ordinary shower, you could try *uma duche hidromassagem* (hydromassage) – one with *jactos multidirecionais* (multidirectional jets) that can pound you from the side. These are not yet widely available, so you may need to ask a local supplier to help you track one down. If you do want one of these, make sure that the water pressure in your area is sufficient to power it properly – and that your cubicle is watertight!

O lavatório – the basin

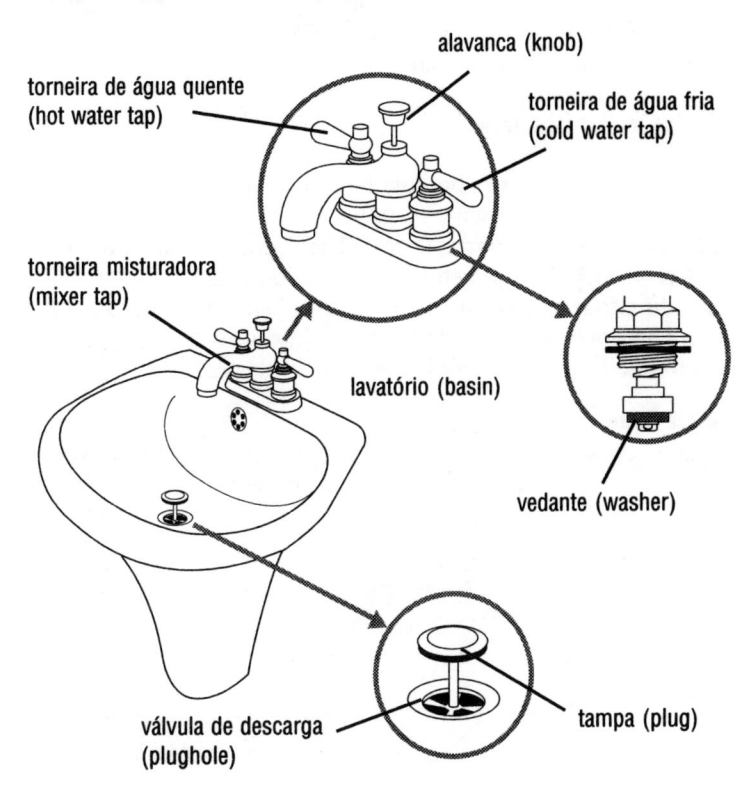

alavanca (knob)

torneira de água quente (hot water tap)

torneira de água fria (cold water tap)

torneira misturadora (mixer tap)

lavatório (basin)

vedante (washer)

válvula de descarga (plughole)

tampa (plug)

Lever operated plughole covers are the norm for basins and baths. Mixer taps are probably more common than in the UK, and there are two kinds: *uma torneira misturadora* has separate hot and cold controls, while *uma torneira com monocomando* has a single lever which controls the volume and temperature.

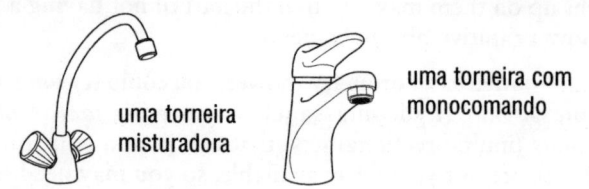

uma torneira misturadora

uma torneira com monocomando

A bacia – washbowl

Instead of a *lavatório* (basin), you could have a *bacia* (bowl) with wall mounted taps. This can be *de bancada* – fitted on top of a vanity unit – or *de embutir* – set into a bathroom unit like a normal basin.

A sanita – the loo

The English sometimes borrow foreign words to refer to things which one doesn't discuss in polite society – 'loo' comes from the French word *l'eau* (the water). The Portuguese are a bit more matter-of-fact, usually referring to the loo as *a sanita* – though they do also have their own euphemistic terms too, and as in the US, when they say *casa de banho* (bathroom), they may mean the toilet. The technology is the same however.

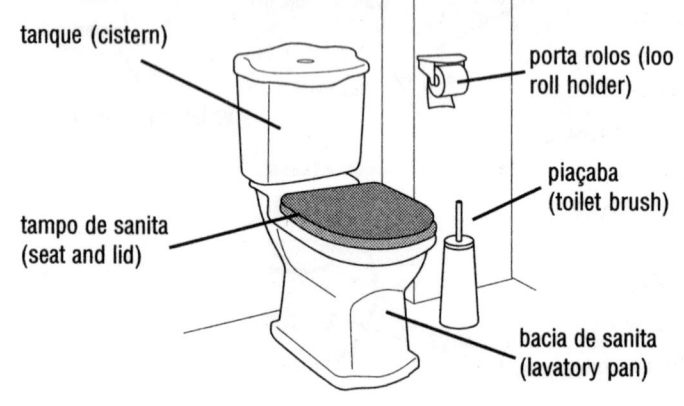

tanque (cistern)

porta rolos (loo roll holder)

piaçaba (toilet brush)

tampo de sanita (seat and lid)

bacia de sanita (lavatory pan)

A casa de banho – bathroom

acessórios (mpl) de casa de banho	bathroom accessories
alavanca (f)	knob/lever
anilha (f)	washer (metal)
armário (m) de casa de banho	bathroom cabinet
armário (m) de medicamentos	medicine cabinet
armário (m) de remédios	medicine cabinet
autoclismo (m)	flush
bacia (f)	washbasin – a normal basin with taps, or one on top of a cupboard or set into a unit
bacia de sanita (f)	toilet bowl
balança (f)	scales
banheira (f)	bathtub
base (f) de chuveiro	shower tray
bidé (m)	bidet
balde de lixo (m)	rubbish bin
balde de lixo com pedal (m)	pedal bin
cabine de duche (f)	shower cubicle
chuveiro (m)	shower
descalcificador (m)	water softener
duche (f)	shower
espelho (m)	mirror
esquentador (m) de água	water heater (gas)
hidromassagem (m)	hydromassage
lavatório (m)	basin
móveis (mpl)	fittings
painel (m) de banheira	shower screen
pano de rosto (m)	facecloth
papel higiénico (m)	toilet paper
piaçaba (f)	toilet brush
porta rolos (m)	loo roll holder
prateleira (f) de vidro	glass shelf

revestimento (m)	surround/splashback
saboneteira (f)	soap dish
sanita (f)	lavatory
sifão (m)	U-bend
sifão (m) de botelha	bottle trap
sifão em S (m)	S-bend
tampa (f)	plug
tampo de sanita (m)	toilet seat/lid
tanque (m)	cistern
termoacumulador	water heater (electric)
toalheiro eléctrico (m)	heated towel rail
toalheiro (m)	towel rail
torneira de água fria (f)	cold water tap
torneira de água quente (f)	hot water tap
torneira misturadora (f)	mixer tap with separate hot/cold water taps
torneira monocomando (f)	mixer tap with combined flow/temperature control
tubos (mpl) de descarga	waste pipes, from basin/bath
válvula de descarga (f)	plughole with lever plug
vedante (m)	sealing washer – the one you change to stop a tap dripping

A cozinha – kitchen

One of the main differences between a Portuguese kitchen and its British counterpart is the oven – or lack of it. The Portuguese are not great roasters or bakers – the frying pan is their weapon of choice, so you may find that your kitchen has a hob but no oven. Other than that, appliances and fittings are much the same.

bacia (f)	bowl of sink
balde de lixo (m)	bin
bancada (f)	work surface
boca (f)	burner in hob (gas)
congelador (m)	freezer
desentupidor (m)	plunger

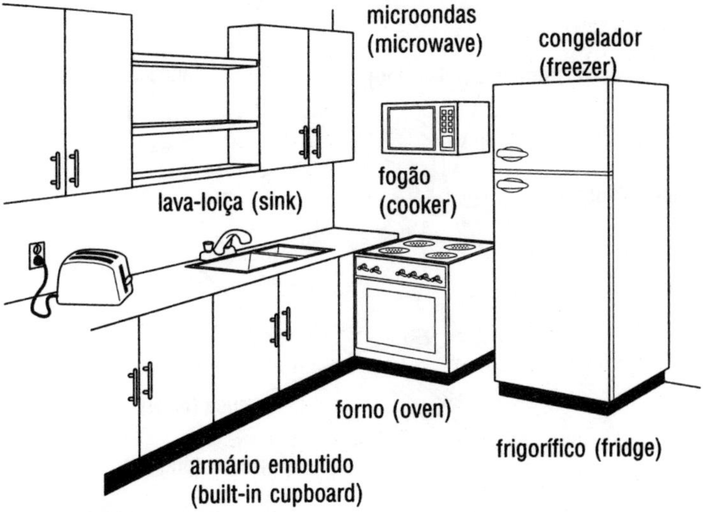
microondas
(microwave)
congelador
(freezer)
fogão
(cooker)
lava-loiça (sink)
forno (oven)
frigorífico (fridge)
armário embutido
(built-in cupboard)

escorredor (m)	drainer/dish rack
exhaustor (m)	cooker hood extractor
fachada (f)	front (doors and drawer)
fogão (m)	cooker
forno (m)	oven
frigorífico (m)	fridge
inox	stainless steel, from *inoxidável* meaning rustproof
ladrão (m)	overflow
lava-loiça (m)	sink
lavandaria (f)	laundry, wash house
máquina de lavar loiça (f)	dishwasher
máquina de lavar roupa (f)	washing machine
máquina de secar roupa (f)	tumble dryer
microondas (m)	microwave
placa (f)	burner in hob (electric)
tampa (f)	plug
tapajuntas (m)	sealing strip (tiles/worksurface)
válvula de descarga (f)	plughole
ventilação (f)	ventilation

O lava-loiça – the sink

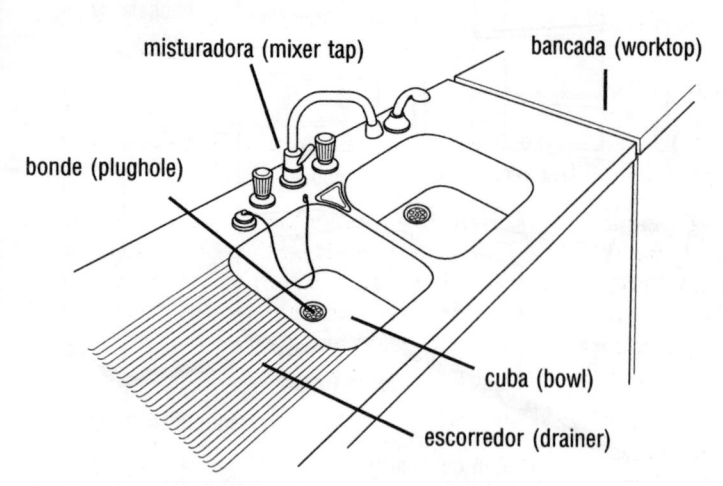

- misturadora (mixer tap)
- bancada (worktop)
- bonde (plughole)
- cuba (bowl)
- escorredor (drainer)

A fossa séptica – the septic tank

If your house is in a rural area, it is likely that it will not be connected to *o esgoto* (mains drains), so you will need *uma fossa séptica* (septic tank) – or a *mini-ETAR* (*Estação de Tratamento de Águas Residuais* – waste water treatment station). If you have an old *fossa*, you may well need a new one – the old ones just store the waste rather than breaking it down and allowing the filtered liquids to soak away into the ground.

But first, what is a *fossa séptica*? They vary, but essentially it is a system of chambers, dug in the ground near the house.

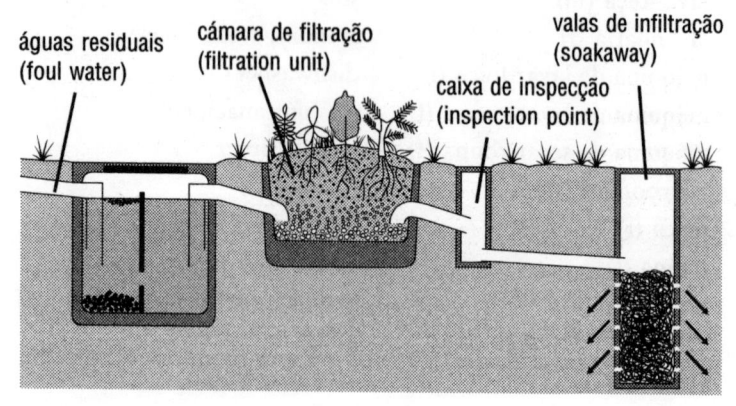

- águas residuais (foul water)
- cámara de filtração (filtration unit)
- valas de infiltração (soakaway)
- caixa de inspecção (inspection point)

The first chamber is a watertight tank into which the sewer and house drains empty foul water. Solid matter is broken down by bacteriological action – a process which takes around a week. Not all solid matter breaks down, and the tank will need emptying out from time to time by a tanker, which takes the remains to proper treatment facilities. The length of time between visits will depend on the size of the tank and how many households are connected to it.

The second chamber is the filtration unit, typically a bed of sand. This may be closed, or capped with earth with grass or small plants growing above. (Trees and bushes must be kept away from *fossas* because their roots can damage the structures.) It may also incorporate an inspection pit to see whether the septic tank is doing its job properly or needs emptying.

The final stage is the *valas de infiltração* (soakaway) – pipes with holes running through a porous bed of rubble or gravel. The filtration unit and soakaway can be combined into one, or if the filtered water can be released into a stream, the soakaway may not be necessary.

A *fossa* system takes some space – a minimum of 150m² free from trees and shrubs. If there isn't that much space available in the garden, then there is an alternative – *uma mini-ETAR* (mini sewage station). This is a motorised system that circulates and aerates the water, to produce a faster breakdown of solids. As it is faster, less storage volume is required, and as it has its own filtration system, the whole structure is far more compact.

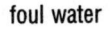

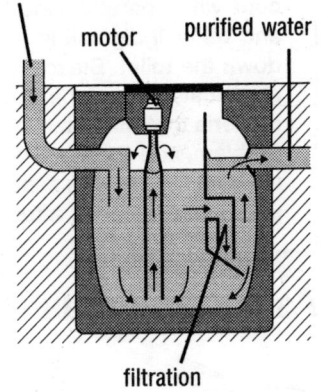

The system may also have a separate grease trap, where grease, oil and other floating nasties will collect at the top, and must be removed periodically. The grease trap may be integral to the *fossa* – but the floating gunge still needs removal.

A new system will have to meet local planning controls and standards on water quality. Talk to the builder and to the *câmara* to work out how large a *fossa* you need, and where – and if – it can be located on your land.

The simplest solution is probably to put the whole business in the hands of a building firm. Most decent builders will be able to construct one for you, though there are also specialist firms about. They will know the ropes, and you'll have to hire them anyway unless you want to dig those holes yourself!

águas residuais (fpl)	waste water
caixa de inspecção (f)	inspection unit
câmara de filtração (f)	filtration unit
fossa séptica (f)	septic tank
lodos (mpl)	sludge
purificação (f)	purification
valas (fpl) de infiltração	soakaway pipes

Fossa-lized flushing!

Fossas sépticas and *mini-ETARs* are organic systems that are designed for dealing with organic matter. They cannot cope with cigarette ends, tampons, *preservativos* (condoms) and other indigestible objects that people routinely flush down the toilet. Bleach, paint, white spirit, and other harsh chemicals cannot be flushed either, as these will kill the bacteria that make the system work. Ordinary soap is not a problem, and there are washing powders and cleaners that are safe for use with septic tanks. Look after your *fossa* and your *fossa* will look after you!

As ferramentas – tools

chave-de-boca inglesa (adjustable spanner)

chave-de-boca spanner

corta-tubos (pipe cutter)

maçarico de brasagem (soldering lamp)

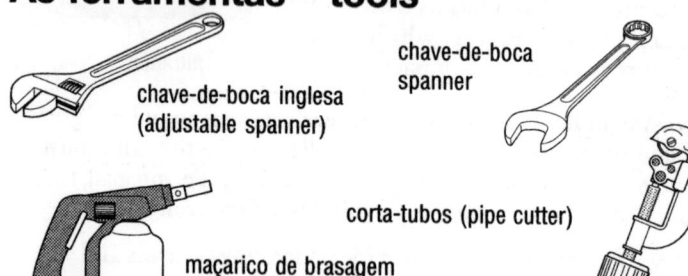

chave-de-boca (inglesa) (f)	(adjustable) spanner
corta-tubos (m)	pipe cutter
desentupidor (m)	plunger
fita (f) teflon	PTFE tape
maçarico (m)	blow lamp
maçarico de brasagem (m)	soldering lamp
serra (f) para metais	hacksaw

> ### The essential plumbing term
> When you need this, you won't have time to learn it, so learn it now.
>
> '*Socorro, há uma fuga de água!*' (Help, there's a leak!)

English – Portuguese quick reference

Pipework – a canalização

cast iron	ferro fundido (m)
copper	cobre (m)
downpipe	tubo de escoamento (m)
drain cock	válvula de descarga (f)
elbow joint	joelho (m)
gutter	canaleira (f)
joint	união (f)/peça (f)
compression	a rosca
soldered	soldada
junction	união (f)
lead	chumbo (m)
mains water	água da rede (f)
pipe	tubo (m), tubulação (f), bicha (f)
pipe clip	abraçadeira (f)
plastic	plástico (m)
regulator	reductor (m) de pressão

stop cock	válvula (f) de fechamento
valve	válvula (f)
waste water system	sistema (m) de águas residuais
water meter	contador (m) de água

Bathroom – a casa de banho

basin	lavatório (m), bacia (f)
bathroom accessories	acessórios (mpl) de banho
bathtub	banheira (f)
cistern	tanque (m)
hydromassage cabinet	duche de hidromassagem (m)
lavatory	sanita (f)
medicine cabinet	armário (m) de remédios
mirror	espelho (m)
mixer tap	torneira misturadora (f), com monocomando (f)
plug	tampa (f)
rubbish bin	balde (m) de lixo
scales	balança (f)
shower	duche (f)
shower cubicle	cabine de ducha (f)
soap dish	saboneteira (f)
tap	torneira (f)
toilet brush	piaçaba (f)
toilet pan	bacia de sanita (f)
toilet roll holder	porta rolo (m)
towel rail / ring	toalheiro (m)
towel rail, heated	toalheiro eléctrico (m)
U-bend	sifão (m)
washer	anilha (f)
waste pipes	tubos (mpl) de esgoto
WC seat lid	tampo (m) de sanita

Kitchen – a cozinha

basin / bowl	bacia (m)
bin	balde (m) de lixo
burner in hob (electric)	placa (f)
burner in hob (gas)	boca (f)
cooker	fogão (m)
cooker hood	exhaustor (m)
dishwasher	máquina (f) de lavar loiça
drainer	escorredor (m)
freezer	congelador (m)
fridge	frigorífico (m)
microwave	microondas (m)
oven	forno (m)
overflow	ladrão (m)
plug	tampa (f)
plughole	válvula de descarga (f)
sink	lava-loiça (m)
sink plunger	desentupidor (m)
stainless steel	inox (m)
tumble dryer	máquina de secar roupa (f)
washing machine	máquina de lavar roupa (f)
work surface	bancada (f)

Septic tank – a fossa séptica

filtration unit	câmara de filtração (f)
inspection unit	caixa de inspecção (f)
purification	purificação (f)
septic tank	fossa séptica (f)
sludge	lodos (mpl)
soakaway pipes	valas (fpl) de infiltração
waste water	águas residuais (fpl)

Tools – as ferramentas

adjustable spanner	chave-de-boca ajustável (f)
blow lamp	maçarico (m)
hacksaw	serra (f) para metais/de arco
pipe cutter	corta-tubos (m)
soldering lamp	maçarico de brasagem (m)
spanner	chave-de-boca (f)

07

o aquecimento e a electricidade – heating and electricity

Almost the same...

Heating and lighting appliances and usages are actually very similar in the UK and Portugal – except of course that you're probably planning on using a lot less central heating!

With electricity, the most obvious difference is that in Portugal there are several levels of power supply, which attract different standing charges and tariffs. Generally, electricity is relatively expensive, and you can expect the odd power cut in rural areas. You should install surge protection and UPS (uninterruptible power supply) if you use a computer for work.

With gas, there is a much more widespread use of bottled or tank gas, because piped gas does not exist outside of Lisbon.

Wood is used more as a fuel outside of towns. Supplies are plentiful, prices are competitive and rural houses generally have the space to store large stocks.

O aquecimento – heating

The first question is, which fuel(s) will you use?

- *lenha* (firewood) is very popular – most rural Portuguese houses have a wood-burning *lareira* (fireplace) or *salamandra* (stove). *Lenha* should be stored for at least a few months before it is needed – green wood produces a lot of tar which condenses in the chimney and creates problems.

- *briquetes* (smokeless fuel briquettes) can be used instead of or with wood. If you want to run central heating from a solid fuel stove, *briquetes* are cleaner-burning and more efficient than wood.

- oil-fired systems are rarely used in Portugal, so you are unlikely to move into a property which has one, and the cost of installing a new one is correspondingly high – while the cost of fuel varies with the price of crude oil.

- *gás* (gas!) – mains gas is available from GDP (Gás de Portugal), but only in Lisbon. Heaters, and even central heating systems, are often run off *garrafas de gás butano* (bottled butane), which is cheap and widely available. If you have space, you can install a large *tanque* (tank), but this is an expensive option – except in the very long term – and can push up your household insurance costs.

* *electricidade* (electricity) is relatively expensive, and is not recommended as a space heating fuel. If you do go electric, you should use *acumuladores de calor* (night-storage heaters) to take advantage of the cheaper night tariff.

* *energia solar* (solar power) is used, mainly for heating water directly. Given that Portugal is not exactly short of sunshine, it is surprising that it is not used more for generating electricity. It is well worth looking at a solar installation for water heating and/or power needs – see page 120.

What is right for you will depend upon the nature of your house and the way that you intend to use it.

* Is there *uma lareira* (fireplace) or can one be installed?

* If the house is in an urban area, are there restrictions on solid fuel fires?

* How much storage space do you have for solid fuel, or for a gas tank?

* Will the house be used mainly in the summer, or at times throughout the year, or will it be your permanent home? If you only need the occasional heating on chilly evenings, the cost and efficiency of the fuel is a minor consideration, and the cost of installation will probably be your main factor.

O aquecimento central – central heating

Central heating generally works by means of *radiadores* (radiators) though *aquecimento do chão* (underfloor heating) is a possible alternative.

A modern Portuguese system is well regulated. A *sensor externo* (external sensor) picks up the outside temperature and adjusts the temperature of the circulating water appropriately. Within the house, a *termostato de quarto* (room thermostat) will control the heat in a zone or room, while a *válvula termostática* (thermostatic regulator) can control individual radiators.

The *caldeira* (boiler) can be *montado à parede* (wall-mounted) or *no chão* (free-standing).

O aquecimento central – central heating

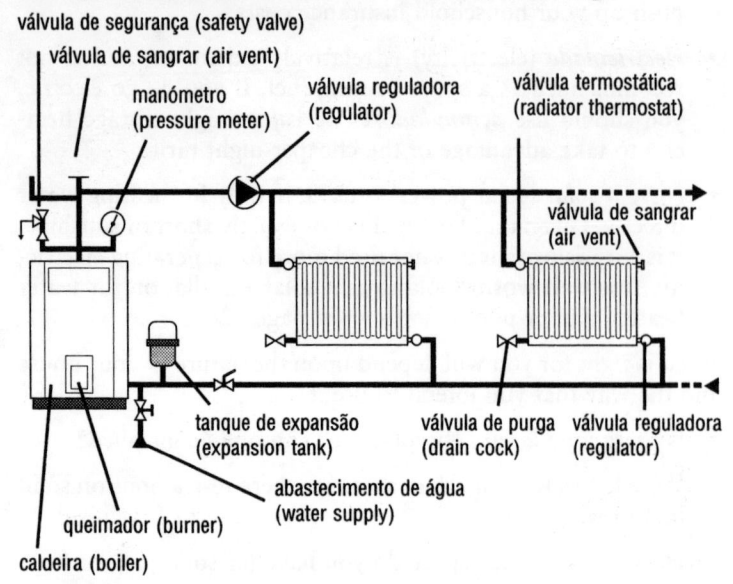

- válvula de segurança (safety valve)
- válvula de sangrar (air vent)
- manómetro (pressure meter)
- válvula reguladora (regulator)
- válvula termostática (radiator thermostat)
- válvula de sangrar (air vent)
- tanque de expansão (expansion tank)
- válvula de purga (drain cock)
- válvula reguladora (regulator)
- abastecimento de água (water supply)
- queimador (burner)
- caldeira (boiler)

A lareira – the fireplace

An open fire is always attractive, and as long as you don't have to do it too often, lumping in the logs or buckets of coal and clearing out the ash can feel more like fun than a chore.

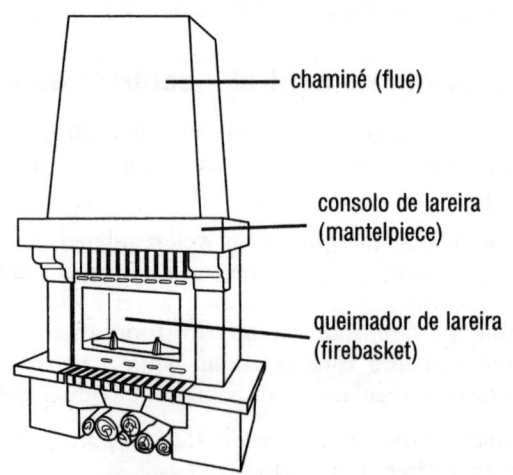

- chaminé (flue)
- consolo de lareira (mantelpiece)
- queimador de lareira (firebasket)

Lareiras can be rather grand, built from thick stone and heavy beams

Os aquecedores – heaters

convector eléctrico
(convector heater)

aquecedor soprador
(blow heater)

acumulador de calor
(storage radiator)

aquecedor eléctrico
(electric fire)

radiador infravermelho
(infra-red heater)

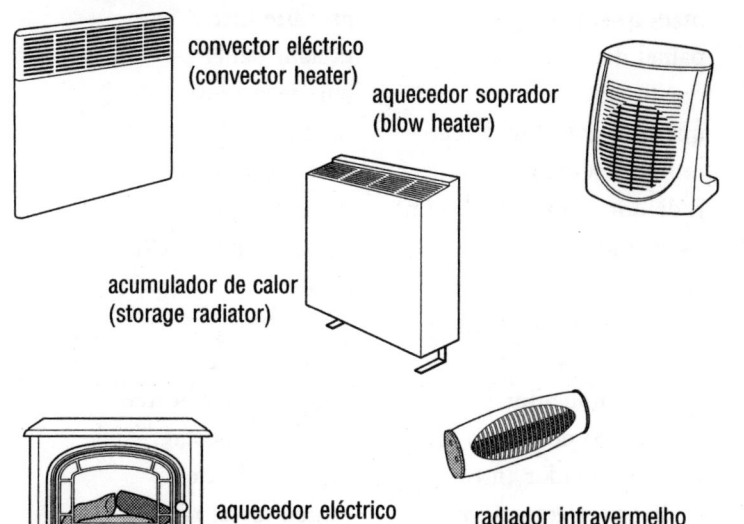

Lexicon: o aquecimento – heating

abastecimento de água (m)	incoming water supply
acumulador de calor (m)	storage radiator
aquecedor eléctrico (m)	electric fire
aquecedor soprador (m)	blow/fan heater
briquetes (mpl)	fuel briquettes
caldeira (f)	boiler
central (m) de aquecimento	heating controls
consolo (m) de lareira	mantelpiece
convector eléctrico (m)	convector heater
depósito (de gás) (m)	tank (for propane)
electricidade (f)	electricity
garrafa (f)	bottle, e.g. for butane
GPL (m)	LPG – liquid propane gas
lenha (f)	firewood

limpa-chaminés (m)	chimneysweep
manómetro (m)	pressure meter
painel de aquecimento (m)	radiant panel
queimador (m)	burner in boiler
queimador (m) de lareira	firebasket
radiador a óleo (m)	oil-filled radiator
radiador infravermelho (m)	infra-red heater
salamandra (f)	wood burning stove
sensor (m)	sensor
tabuleiro (m) para cinzas	cinder tray
tanque (m) de expansão	expansion tank
termoacumulador (m)	electric water-heater
termostato de quarto (m)	room thermostat
termoventilador (m)	blow/fan heater
toalheiro eléctrico (m)	heated towel rail
válvula (f)	valve
válvula de purga	drain cock
válvula de sangrar	bleeder valve, at the highest point for venting a system, or on a radiator
válvula de segurança	safety valve
válvula reguladora	regulator/stop cock on radiator
válvula termostática	radiator thermostat

Heating and lightning

If you have a propane tank it must be earthed. Some friends, enjoying a dramatic thunderstorm one night, watched in horror as lightning struck their oil tank. It glowed bright blue, but fortunately nothing else happened! They had a lightning conductor fitted the next day.

Their luck didn't hold though that night – another strike fried their TV, video, satellite box and most of the telephone wiring and sockets in the house.

O abastecimento de electricidade – the electricity supply

If you are having your electrical supply installed or reinstalled, you will have to decide which *potência* (power supply level) will best suit. There are several possible power ratings, ranging upwards from 3kW. This would probably suffice for a holiday home with low power needs, but you'll need more like 9kW to 12kW if you're going to spend more time there.

- 6kW will be enough to power simultaneously the lights, three or four small appliances, e.g. TV, fridge, hoover, and a single more power-hungry appliance such as a washing machine or an electric cooker.

- 9kW will also handle a second large appliance.

- 12kW is the minimum if electricity is also used for heating, and would be sufficient for a house of up to 100m².

- 15kW will handle the power and heating for a larger house.

You would only need to go above that if you have a very large, all-electric house, or you use heavy machinery in your work.

The incoming electricity supply, up to the *contador (*meter) and the *disjuntor principal* (mains switch), is the responsibility of the supply company.

Monophase and triphase

In Portugal, there are two distinct types of electricity supply. *Monofase* current is much the same as domestic supply in the UK: 50Hz AC at 220 volts (ours is 240 volts, but the difference does not affect normal appliances). *Trifase* supplies both 220 and 380 volts, and is mainly designed for industrial use. It's what's usually supplied to farms to power their machinery, so if your house is in the countryside, it may be what is supplied to you. If you have a 18kW or higher *potência*, it will be supplied as *trifase*.

In practice, having *trifase* doesn't create any problems, but it does entail a higher tariff – if you don't need it for heavy machinery, get your supplier to put you back onto *monofase*.

Os fusíveis e os disjuntores – fuses and circuit breakers

A modern *quadro eléctrico* (distribution board) doesn't have *fusíveis* (fuses), but instead has a *disjuntor* (circuit breaker) on each branch. The best *disjuntores* are the differential variety, which give greater protection against electric shocks. They have a normal magno-thermal cut-out which is triggered by a surge in the voltage or a short circuit, and a cut-out which is triggered if there is an earth fault anywhere in the circuit (e.g. from a faulty shaver to the bathroom floor, via you and your wet feet).

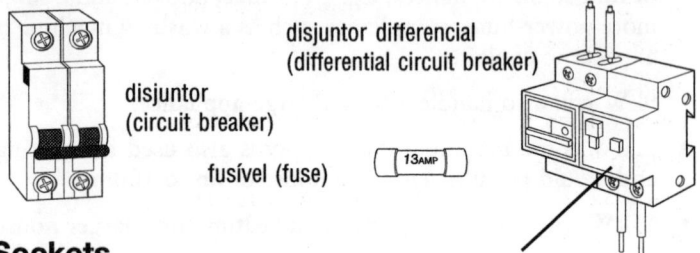

disjuntor differencial
(differential circuit breaker)

disjuntor
(circuit breaker)

fusível (fuse)   13AMP

Sockets

Modern Portuguese *tomadas de corrente* (electric sockets) have two round holes for the *fase* (live) and *neutro* (neutral) pins, plus a round earth pin. Older sockets may just have the live and neutral holes, and older plugs will match. Most new appliances have a plug with a hole for the socket's earth pin, though some – lamps, for instance, and also appliances designed to fit shaver sockets – will just have the two pins.

UK 240 volt appliances will work perfectly well on Portuguese 220 volt supply – as long as you have plug adaptors – but it's easier to buy Portuguese. You don't have the plug problem and it's easier to take it back if it doesn't work.

A electricidade – electricity

adaptor (m) multi-socket
abastecimento de electricidade electrical supply
cabo (m) cable
contador (m) meter
corrente alternada (f) AC

corrente continua (f)	DC
corrente eléctrica (f)	electric current
curto-circuito (m)	short circuit
disjuntor (m)	circuit breaker
disjuntor magno-térmico (m)	circuit breaker
disjuntor differencial (m)	differential cut-out
disjuntor principal (m)	mains supply switch
fase (f)	live wire
ficha (f)	plug
fio (m)	cord, lead, wire
fio fusível (m)	wire fuse
fusível (m)	fuse
fusível de cartucho	cartridge fuse
neutro (m)	neutral wire
potência (f)	power level
queimar os fusíveis (v)	blow the fuses
terra (f)	earth
tomada (com terra) (f)	socket (with earth connectors)
voltagem (f)	voltage

Os aquecedores de água – water heaters

There are two main types of *aquecedor*: *esquentadores* – on-demand boilers, either gas or electric, which are all but identical to those in the UK – and the electric *termoacumuladores* (immersion heaters), which are different to the UK variety.

These slim cylinders are wall-mounted or free-standing, depending on size, and almost always in white enamel. The power of the heating element varies, but most are designed to slowly heat a full tank overnight, using cheap-rate electricity. They are also available with a rapid heating option, but check what *potência* your electricity is supplied at – the rapid heaters have a 12kW heating element.

termoacumulador (electric immersion heater)

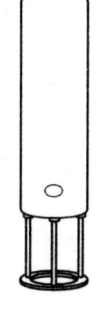

Os electrodomésticos – electrical appliances

The electrical appliances are broadly the same in Portugal and the UK – hardly surprising as they are mostly from the same firms. You may have to hunt around a little to find *uma chaleira* (kettle), as they are not regularly used by the Portuguese. Well, if you don't drink tea and you have a *cafeteira* and a *saca-rolhos* (corkscrew), what's the point of a kettle?

Os electrodomésticos – electrical appliances

altifalante (m)	speaker
amplificador (m)	amplifier
aquecedor (m) de água	water heater
aspirador (m)	vacuum cleaner
atendedor (m) de chamadas	answering machine
batedeira (f)	food mixer
cafeteira (f)	coffee maker
câmara (f) de filmar	video camera
cassete (m)	tape deck
cave (m) de vinhos	(electric) wine cabinet, controlled temperature and humidity
chaleira (m)	kettle
coluna (f)	speaker (column speaker with separate woofer and tweeter)
combi (m)	integrated audio-visual appliance – e.g. TV with built-in video/DVD player
computador (m)	micro computer, PC
congelador (m)	freezer
digital	digital
ecrã (m)	screen
ecrã LCD	LCD screen
ecrã panorâmico	widescreen
ecrã plano	flat screen
ecrã plasma	plasma screen

fogão (cooker)

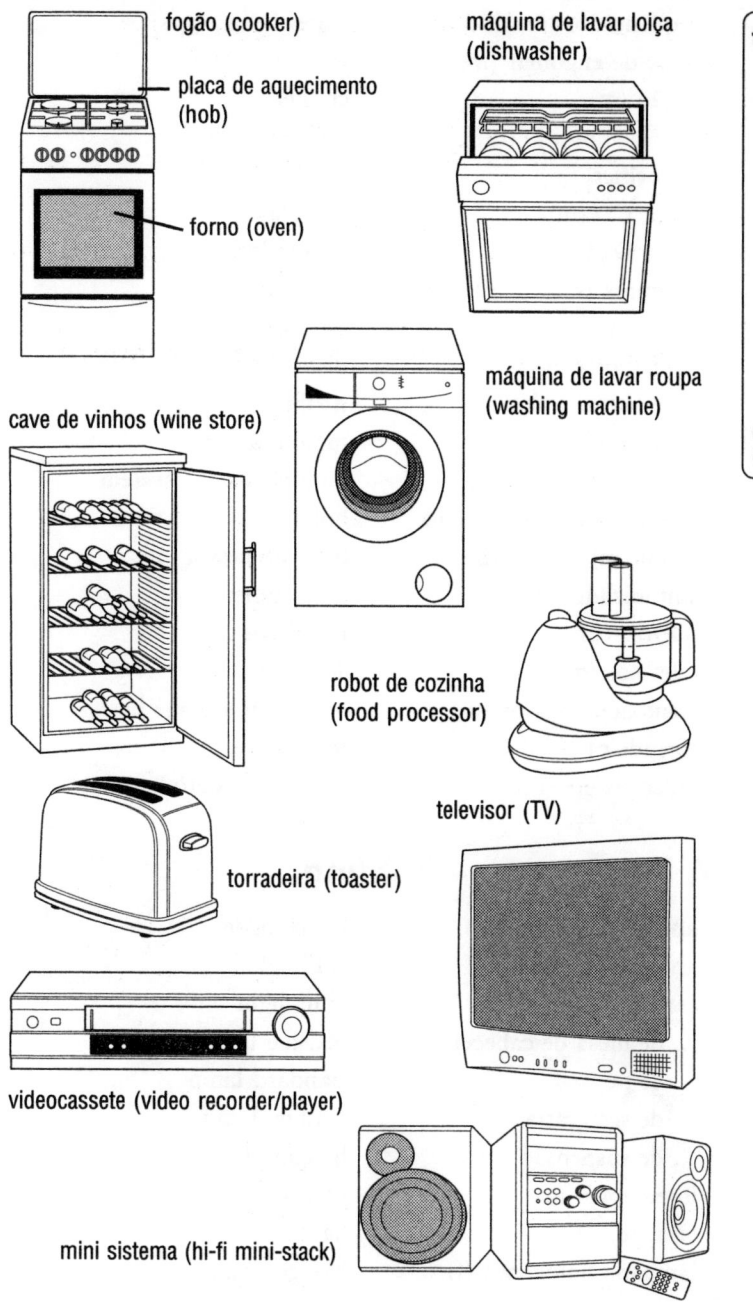

placa de aquecimento (hob)

máquina de lavar loiça (dishwasher)

forno (oven)

cave de vinhos (wine store)

máquina de lavar roupa (washing machine)

robot de cozinha (food processor)

torradeira (toaster)

televisor (TV)

videocassete (video recorder/player)

mini sistema (hi-fi mini-stack)

117 heating and electricity 07

esquentador (m) de água	water heater (gas)
ferro de engomar (m)	iron
fogão (m)	cooker
forno embutido (m)	built-in oven
frigorífico (m)	fridge
leitor CD (m)	CD player
leitor DVD (m)	DVD player
máquina (f)	machine
... de café	espresso machine
... de lavar loiça	dishwasher
... de lavar roupa	washing machine
... de secar roupa	tumble dryer
mini sistema (m)	mini hi-fi stack system
placa (f) de aquecimento	hob
robot (m) de cozinha	food processor
sintonizador (m)	radio tuner
telefone (m)	telephone
televisor (m)	TV
termoacumulador (m)	hot water storage heater
torradeira (f)	toaster
videocassete (m)	video recorder/player

A iluminação – lighting

abajur (m)	lamp shade
aplique (m)	wall light
candeeiro (m)	lamp/light
... de mesa de cabeceira	bedside light
... de pé	standard lamp
... de secretária	reading lamp
... de suspensão	hanging light
interruptor (m)	light switch
lâmpada (f)	light bulb
lâmpada halogénea (f)	halogen bulb

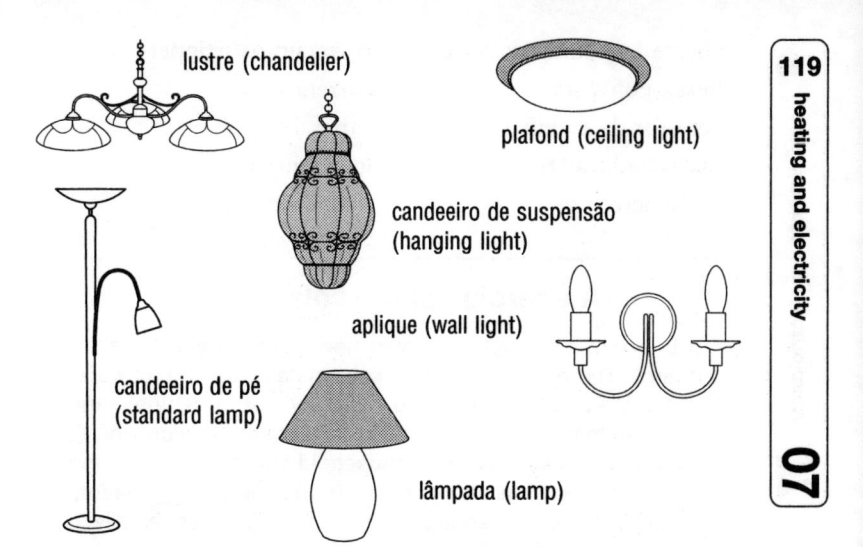

lustre (chandelier)

plafond (ceiling light)

candeeiro de suspensão (hanging light)

aplique (wall light)

candeeiro de pé (standard lamp)

lâmpada (lamp)

lustre (m)	multi-bulb light, chandelier
luz (f)	light (as in the rays of light, not the thing which emits them!)?
plafond (m)	ceiling light
projector (m)	spotlight
régua (f) de 3/4 projectores	strip with 3/4 spot lights
suporte (m) de lâmpada	light socket
tubo fluorescente (m)	fluorescent light

As ferramentas – tools

There are few special tools for electrical work – although they make electrician's versions of hammers, chisels, screwdrivers and other tools.

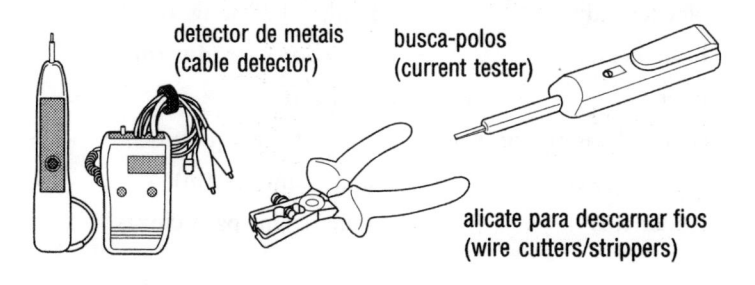

detector de metais (cable detector)

busca-polos (current tester)

alicate para descarnar fios (wire cutters/strippers)

alicate (m) para descarnar fios wire cutters/strippers
busca-polos (m) current tester
detector de metais (m) cable detector
fita isoladora (f) insulating tape
multímetro (m) multimeter

A energia solar – solar energy

It is a common myth that you need a lot of sun for solar energy. There are two kinds of solar installation – direct water heating systems (which do need lots of sunshine), and photovoltaic cells for generating electricity (which don't). Even in the UK an average household can generate around 75% of its electrical energy needs from a rooftop installation. So in Portugal, you should be more than fine – especially in the sun-soaked south!

Termoacumuladores solares (direct water heating systems) are not too expensive to install and are likely to suffice for the needs of a holiday home. For long-term residents, it's worth considering *um sistema fotovoltaico* – although the cost of installation is higher, it will save you money in the long term. Renewable energy is also being promoted by national and international authorities keen to address climate change, so there may be EU or government grants available in your area.

English – Portuguese quick reference

Heating – o aquecimento

bleeder valve	válvula (f) de sangrar
blow heater	aquecedor soprador (m)
boiler	caldeira (f)
central heating controls	central (f) de aquecimento
chimneysweep	limpa-chaminés (m)
cinder tray	tabuleiro (m) para cinzas

convector heater	convector eléctrico (m)
electric fire	lareira eléctrica (f)
firebasket	queimador (f) de lareira
firewood	lenha (f)
fuel briquettes	briquetes (mpl)
heated towel rail	toalheiro eléctrico (m)
infra-red heater	radiador infravermelho (m)
radiator	radiador (m)
radiator thermostat	válvula termostática (f)
sensor	sensor (f)
storage radiator	termoacumulador (m)
stove	salamandra (f)

Electricity – a electricidade

AC	corrente alternada (f)
blow the fuses	queimar os fusíveis
circuit breaker	disjuntor (m)
distribution board	quadro eléctrico (m)
earth (wire)	terra (f)
electric current	corrente eléctrica (f)
electrical supply	abastecimento (m) de electricidade
fuse	fusível (m)
fuse wire	fio fusível (m)
fuse, cartridge	fusível de cartucho (m)
live wire	fase (f)
mains switch	disjuntor principal (m)
meter	contador (m)
neutral wire	neutro (m)
plug	ficha (f)
power level	potência (f)
short circuit	curto-circuito (m)

socket	tomada (f) de corrente
voltage	voltagem (f)

Electrical appliances – os electrodomésticos

amplifier	amplificador (m)
answering machine	atendedor (m) de chamadas
CD player	leitor CD (m)
coffee machine	máquina (f) de café
computer	computador (m)
cooker	fogão (m)
digital	digital
dishwasher	máquina de lavar loiça (f)
distribution board	caixa de distribuição (f)
DVD player	leitor DVD (m)
flat screen (LCD/plasma)	ecrã plana (LCD/plasma)
food mixer	batideira (f)
food processor	robot (m) de cozinha
freezer	congelador (m)
fridge	frigorífico (m)
hob	placa (f) de aquecimento
iron	ferro de engomar (m)
kettle	chaleira (f)
mini hi-fi stack system	mini sistema (m)
oven	forno (m)
radio tuner	sintonizador (m)
speaker	altifalante (m), coluna (f)
telephone	telefone (m)
toaster	torradeira (f)
tumble dryer	máquina de secar roupa (f)
TV	televisor (m)
vacuum cleaner	aspirador (m)

video camera	câmara (f) de filmar
video recorder/player	videocassete (m)
washing machine	máquina de lavar roupa (f)
widescreen	ecrã panorâmico (m)
wine cabinet	cave (f) de vinhos

Lighting – a iluminação

bedside light	lâmpada (f) de mesa de cabeceira
bulb	lâmpada (f)
ceiling light	plafond (m)
chandelier	lustre (f)
fluorescent light	tubo fluorescente (m)
hanging light	candeeiro (m) de suspensão
lamp	lâmpada (f)
lamp shade	quebra-luz (m), ajatur (m)
light	luz (f)
light socket	suporte (m) de lâmpada
light switch	interruptor (m)
lighting	iluminação (f)
reading lamp	candeeiro (m) de secretária
spot light	projector (m)
wall light	aplique (m)

08 a decoração – decorating

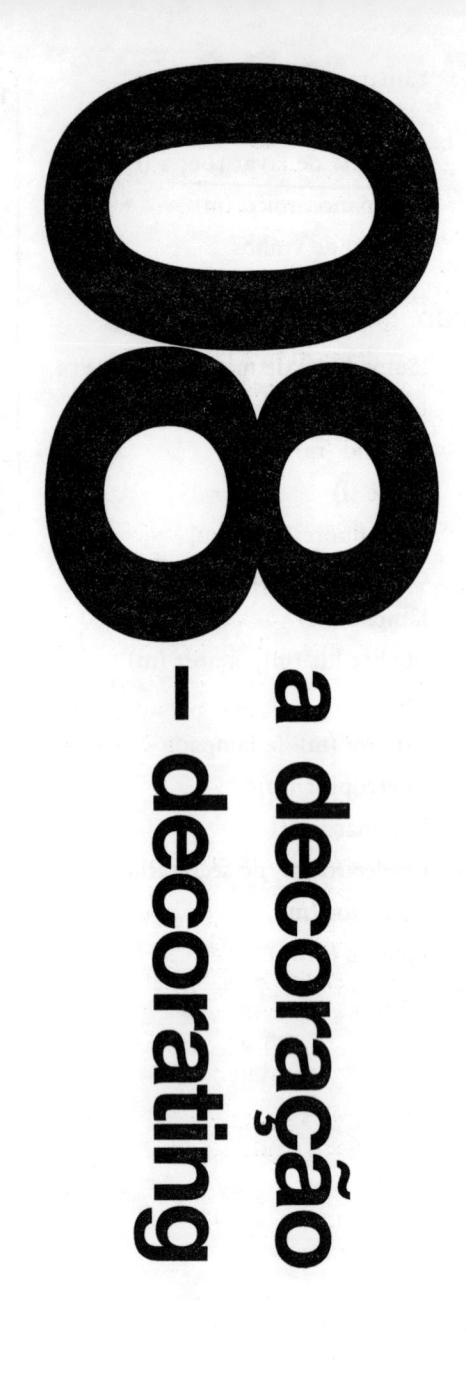

Almost the same...

Portuguese style in decoration and furnishings is not enormously different to ours. Obviously, you will find a huge variety and range of styles in people's houses in Portugal, just as you will in the UK, and these ranges very largely overlap. You will find plenty of modern-styled houses and apartments whose interiors are virtually indistinguishable from their UK counterparts (at the time of writing, IKEA only has one store, just outside Lisbon – but more will surely come!). But they do seem to have a tendency to go that extra mile in terms of ornate patterns, intricate mouldings or gold braiding, so you may have to shop around a bit to find furnishings to your taste.

Some things are different for practical purposes. We have carpets in the UK to keep our feet warm and stop those chilly draughts whistling up through the floorboards – not much need for that when it's 35°C outside; in fact what you want is a nice stone tiled floor to cool your roasting toes on. The change in climate, in vista, in the pace of life may all contribute to you adopting some elements of local style into your plans – but in the end, it's your house, and it should look the way you want it to. The chances are, you'll find what you're after – if you hunt long and hard enough.

Check at the câmara

- If you are thinking about painting the outside walls or the shutters, look around at your neighbours' houses first. If they all use the same colours, or a very restricted range of colours, the area may have rules on external decorations. In this case, ask at the *câmara* before you paint anything. It won't take long, and it could save you days of repainting.

- Likewise, if you live within sight of a historic building, check at the *câmara* before you paint the outside.

A pintura – paint

Portuguese paint is much the same as in the UK – you get the same types in the same sized tins (no surprise there, it's mostly made by the same companies!). The colour range may be a little unfamiliar, but let's face it – you can't really go by the names of colours in English anyway. What colour *is* 'summer orchard haze', exactly? Or 'millpond mist' or 'berry glow'? The only sure way to get the paint you want is to make liberal use of colour cards and tester pots, just as it is over here.

The general words you need for paint are *tinta plástica* for emulsion and *esmalte* or *de óleo* for oil-based paints. Other types of paints include *acrílica* (acrylic), *vinílica* (vinyl), *microporoso* (micro-porous for external woodwork), and *poliuretano* (polyurethane – tough and waterproof), as well as special paints for *piscinas* (swimming pools) and *fachadas* (exterior walls).

O acabamento (the finish) can be *mate* (matt), *acetinado* (satin), or *brilhante* (gloss).

acabamento (m)	finish, e.g. matt/satin
acetinado	satin finish
acrílica	acrylic
aerossol (m)	aerosol
aguarrás (f)	white spirit
brilhante	gloss
esmalte (m)	enamel or oil based paint
mate	matt
microporoso	microporous
pintura (f)	painting / paintwork
primário (m)	primer
primeira mão (f)	first coat
subcapa (f)	undercoat
tinta (f)	paint
tinta de óleo	oil-based paint
tinta para fachadas	exterior wall paint
tinta para pavimento	floor paint
tinta plástica	emulsion
velatura de madeira (f)	wood stain
verniz (m)	varnish

As ferramentas – tools

andaime (m)	scaffold
brocha (f)	round paintbrush
cabo extensível (m)	telescopic handle (for roller)
cavalete (m)	trestle
fita de proteção adesiva (f)	masking tape
pincel (m)	small brush (mostly round)
pistola (f) de pintar	spray gun
rolo (anti-gota) (m)	roller
tábua (f)	board to make a platform on top of two trestles
tabuleiro de pintor (m)	paint tray
toldo de plástico (m)	plastic dust sheet
trapo (m)	rag
trincha (f)	paintbrush

Round brushes

Round paint brushes are much more popular in Portugal than they are in the UK. You have to adjust your technique a little, but the cone-shaped end allows you to get a good edge.

Os revestimentos de paredes – wall coverings

The Portuguese, especially in the South, rarely use any kind of wall coverings other than plaster and paint, so you may find a restricted selection of wall coverings.

In new properties, with fresh, smooth plaster, paint can give an excellent finish, but in older houses *papel de parede* (wallpaper) or *um revestimento textil* (textile wall covering) both have the advantage of covering up minor imperfections without all the filling and smoothing you'd have to do before painting.

You may also come across *tecido de vidro* (glass fibre wall covering). This is a tough alternative to lining paper that can give a smooth finish to cracked walls and ceilings (only minor cracks – it won't hold rotting plaster together). Glass fibre for walls is more commonly found in small quantities or as an adhesive tape for patching up – stick it over a crack in the plaster to help prevent it re-opening in future, then paint or cover as usual.

cola (f)	paste
cola de tapeceiro	wallpaper paste
papel (m) de forro	lining paper
papel (m) de parede	wallpaper
papel (m) pré-colado	ready-pasted wallpaper
papel (m) vinílico	vinyl wallpaper
placa de cortiça (f)	cork tile
revestimento (m) de paredes	wall covering
tecido de vidro (m)	glass fibre wall covering

Os revestimentos texteis – wall textiles

Instead of wallpaper, you could decorate your walls with some kind of *tecido* (textile). If these are natural fibres, e.g. cotton or silk, the sheets must be fitted onto battens, with a polystyrene or other thick liner. Synthetics can also be hung this way, but can also by pasted directly onto the wall.

algodão (m)	cotton
sarapilheira (f)	hessian
feltro (m)	felt
flanela (f)	flannel
lã (f)	wool
seda (f)	silk
tecido (m)	fabric
veludo (m)	velvet

As ferramentas – tools

brocha de cola (f)	pasting brush
cordel (m)	string

brocha de cola (pasting brush)
tesoura (scissors)
fita métrica (measuring tape)
prumo (plumb line)
nível de bolha (spirit level)
rolo para uniões (seam roller)

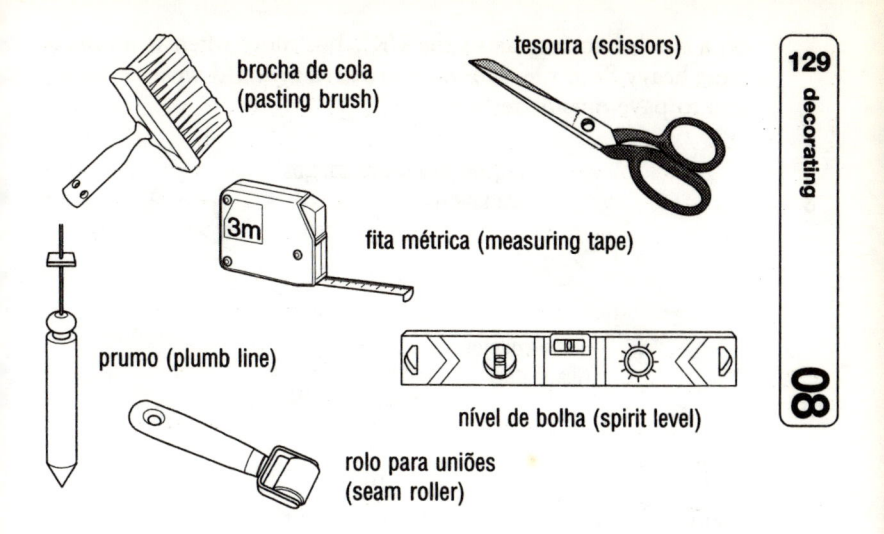

desempenadeira (f)	wallpaper smoother
escova seca (f)	wallpaper brush
esponja (f)	sponge
espátula (f)	filling knife
faca universal (f)	Stanley knife
fita métrica (f)	measuring tape
máquina (f) de vapor	steamer (for removing old paper)
mesa de passar cola (f)	pasting table
nível (m) de bolha	spirit level
prumo (m)	plumb line
raspadeira de papel de parede	paper stripper
rolo (m) para uniões	seam roller
tesoura (f)	scissors

Colocar azulejos – tiling

As in many parts of Europe, Portuguese bathrooms tend to be completely tiled. You'll need *azulejos* for the walls and *pavimento* for the floor – and of course they'll need to be *impermeáveis* (waterproof). Watch out for the Portuguese word *mosaico* – it may sometimes refer to mosaic tiles (usually supplied in sheets on a mesh backing, as in the UK), but more often it means a large heavy floor tile. *Mosaicos* are used for hard-wearing floors and to pave outside terraces.

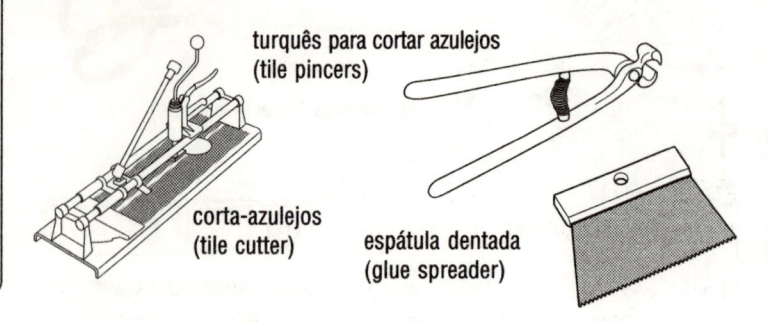

turquês para cortar azulejos (tile pincers)

corta-azulejos (tile cutter)

espátula dentada (glue spreader)

azulejo (m)	tile
azulejo cerâmico	ceramic tile
azulejo espelho	mirror tile
azulejo de parede	wall tile
cimento-cola (m)	tile cement
corta-azulejos (m)	tile cutter
espátula dentada (f)	glue spreader
pavimentos (mpl)	floor tiles
placa de cortiça (f)	cork tile
turquês (m) para cortar azulejos	tile pincers

Os revestimentos de chãos – floor coverings

The Portuguese simply do not use carpets and vinyls as much as we do, so don't expect to find the same choices or the same prices. They have gone for wood laminates in a big way, just as we have in the UK, so there's plenty of those around. But the traditional Portuguese house has tiled floors in the kitchen, bathroom, conservatory and similar hard-worn places, and a lot of solid parquet elsewhere. Learn from the locals. They have been living with their climate all their lives. Bare tiled and wood floor are cooler in the summer and easy to keep clean all year round.

| carpete (m) | carpet |
| lamparquete (m) | wood effect laminate flooring |

parquete (m)	wood flooring (solid/laminate)
parquete mosaico (m)	small wooden tiles in patterns, supplied on a mesh backing
parquete tradicional (m)	blocks of solid wood
revestimento de vinil (m)	vinyl flooring (lino)
tapete (m)	rug

As cortinas e os estores – curtains and blinds

If you have shutters, you don't need any curtains, except perhaps net ones to give you some privacy when the shutters and windows are open – though that doesn't mean that you can't have them if you want them. They can be a key part of a decorative scheme, and can improve the acoustics of a room.

Inward-opening windows may make it difficult to hang curtains, but they make it almost impossible to fit blinds across the whole aperture. The simple solution is to fit slim blinds directly to the windows.

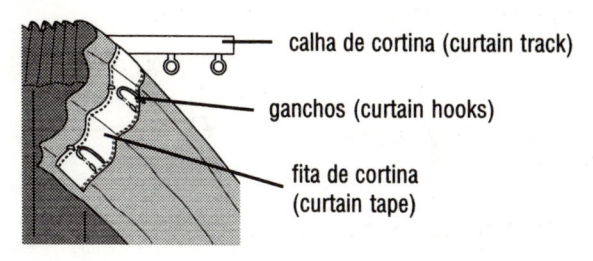

- calha de cortina (curtain track)
- ganchos (curtain hooks)
- fita de cortina (curtain tape)

calha (f) de cortina	curtain track
cortina (f)	curtain
cortinas de tule	net curtains
estore (m)	blind
estore de enrolar (m)	roller blind
estore veneziano (m)	venetian blind
fita (f) de cortina	curtain tape
ganchos (mpl)	curtain hooks
láminas (fpl)	slats on blind

roletes (fpl)	curtain runners
sanefa (f)	curtain pelmet
suportes (mpl)	wall/window fittings for blind
tule (m)	netting
varão (m) de cortina	curtain pole

Os móveis – furniture

A sala de jantar e a sala de estar – the dining room and living room

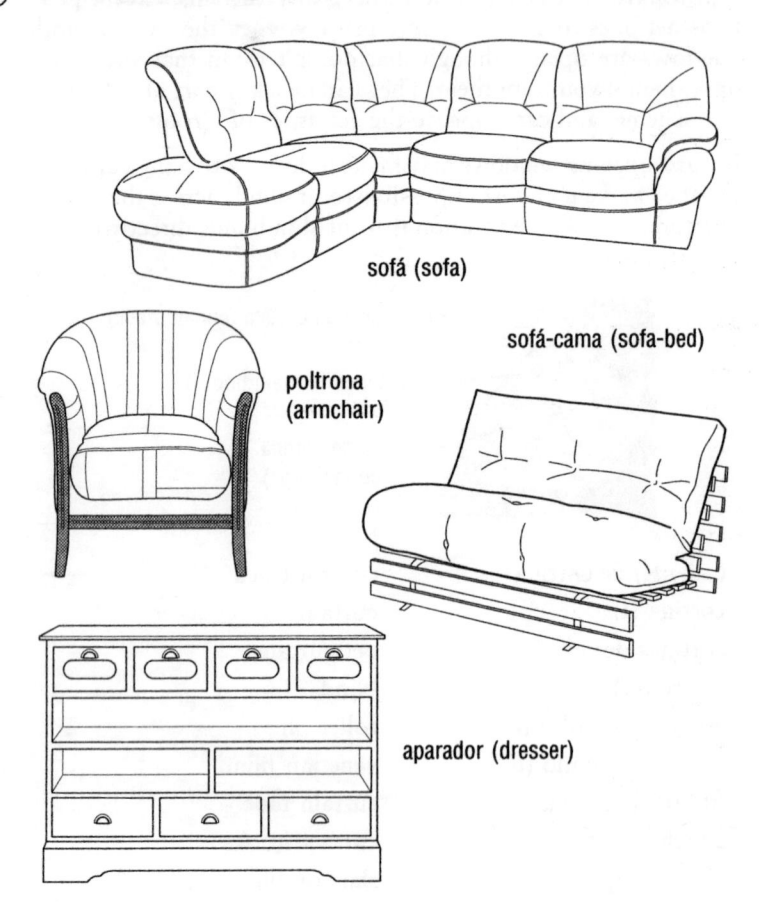

sofá (sofa)

poltrona (armchair)

sofá-cama (sofa-bed)

aparador (dresser)

O quarto (de dormir) – the bedroom

lâmpara de cabeceira (bedside light)

cômoda (chest of drawers)

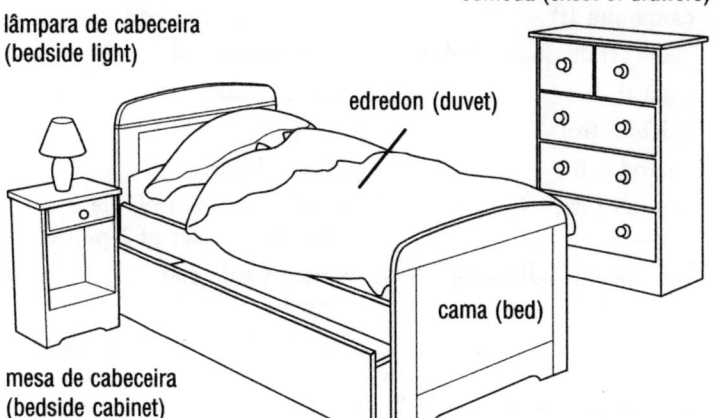

edredon (duvet)

cama (bed)

mesa de cabeceira (bedside cabinet)

cama-alta (raised bed)

baú (chest)

almofada (f)	pillow, cushion
aparador (m)	sideboard/dresser
armário (f)	cupboard
armário de TV/hi-fi	TV/hi-fi cabinet
assento (m)	seat
banco (m)	bench
baú (m)	chest
beliche (m)	bunk bed
bufete (m)	sideboard
cadeira (f)	chair

cadeirão (m)	armchair
cama (f)	bed
cama-alta (f)	raised platform bed
cama (f) de quatro colunas	four-poster bed
cana (f)	cane, rattan
colchão (m)	mattress
cômoda (f)	chest of drawers
conjunto de... (m)	set of, e.g. *conjunto de 2 almofadas* = set of 2 pillows
conjunto de sofás (m)	suite of sofa and armchairs
cristaleira (f)	display cabinet for glassware
edredon (m)	duvet
estante (f)	set of shelves
estante (f) de livros	bookcase
guarda-roupa (m)	wardrobe
lâmpada de cabeceira (f)	bedside light
mesa (f)	table
mesa de apoio	occasional table
mesa de centro	coffee table
mesa de cabeceira	bed side cabinet
poltrona (f)	armchair
prateleira (f)	shelf
sofá (m)	sofa
sofá-cama (m)	sofa-bed
toucador (m)	dressing table

English – Portuguese quick reference

A pintura – paint

brush, flat	trincha (f)
brush, round	brocha (f)
brush, small	pincel (m)
dust sheet (plastic)	toldo (de plástico) (m)

emulsion	tinta plástica (f)
gloss	brilhante
house paint	pintura (f) para fachadas
masking tape	fita de protecção adesiva (f)
oil-based paint	esmalte (m)
paint	tinta (f)
paintwork	pintura (f)
paint tray	tabuleiro de pintor (m)
primer	primário (m)
rag	trapo (m)
roller	rolo (m)
turpentine	aguarrás (f)
undercoat	subcapa (f)
varnish	verniz (m)
wood stain	velatura de madeira (m)

Os revestimentos de paredes – wall coverings

cork tile	placa de cortiça (f)
filling knife	espátula (f)
measuring tape	fita métrica (f)
paper stripper	raspadeira (f) de papel de parede
pasting brush	brocha de cola (f)
pasting table	mesa (f) de passar cola
plumb line	prumo (m)
scissors	tesoura (f)
seam roller	rolo (m) de uniões
spirit level	nível (m) de bolha
sponge	esponja (f)
Stanley knife	faca universal (f)
string	cordel (m)
textile / fabric	tecido (m)
vinyl wallpaper	papel (m) de parede vinílico
wallpaper	papel (m) de parede

wallpaper brush	escova seca (f)
wallpaper paste	cola (f) de tapeceiro
wallpaper smoother	desempenadeira (f)
wallpaper, ready-pasted	papel pré-colado (m)

Colocar azulejos – tiling

ceramic tile	azulejo cerâmico (m)
floor tile	pavimento (m) / mosaico (m)
glue spreader	espátula dentada (f)
mirror tile	azulejo espelho (m)
paving slab	mosaico (m)
tile	azulejo (m)
tile cement	cimento-cola (m), argamassa (f)
tile cutter	corta-azulejos (m)
tile pincers	turquês (m) para cortar azulejos

Os revestimentos de chãos – floor coverings

carpet	carpete (m)
laminate flooring	lamparquete (m)
parquet	parquete tradicional (m)
rug	tapete (m)
vinyl flooring	revestimento de vinil (m)
wood flooring	parquete (m)
wood mosaic flooring	parquete mosaico (m)

As cortinas e os estores – curtains and blinds

blind	estore (m)
curtain	cortina (f)
curtain hooks	ganchos (mpl)
curtain pelmet	sanefa (f)
curtain rod	varão (m) de cortina
curtain runners	roletes (mpl)
curtain tape	fita de cortina (f)

curtain track	calha de cortina (m)
netting	tule (m)
net curtains	cortina de tule (m)

Os móveis – furniture

armchair	poltrona (f), cadeirão (m)
bed	cama (f)
bed side cabinet	mesa de cabeceira (f)
bedside light	lâmpada de mesa de cabeceira (f)
bench	banco (m)
bookcase	estante (f) de livros
chair	cadeira (f)
chest	baú (m)
chest of drawers	cômoda (f)
coffee table	mesa (f) de centro
cupboard	armário (m)
cushion	almofada (f)
dresser	aparador (m)
dressing table	toucador (m)
duvet	edredon (m)
mattress	colchão (m)
pillow	almofada (f)
seat	assento (m)
set of shelves	estante (f)
shelf	prateleira (f)
sideboard	aparador (m) / bufete (m)
sofa	sofá (m)
sofa-bed	sofá-cama (m)
table	mesa (f)
TV/hi-fi cabinet	armário de TV/hi-fi
wardrobe	guarda-roupa (m), roupeiro (m)

09
o jardim –
the garden

Almost the same...

The quintessential 'English country garden' and the Englishman's love of a well-tended lawn are well-known abroad. However, trying to reproduce that during a long hot summer in Portugal will not be easy – you are into a different climate here, a different eco-system – and a different approach to gardens.

In much of Portugal it's too hot and dry to keep a lawn green through the summer without regular watering. If you don't have your own spring or well, you'll be paying for every drop of water used by the *aspersor* (sprinkler) – and that's assuming you're allowed to use it. There are often hosepipe bans during dry spells. Besides, will you be there to water it and cut it? If not, who is going to be there to look after it for you, and at what cost? For most people buying a home in an *urbanização*, this won't present a real problem – communal garden areas will be tended by contractors under the terms of your service charge. The only thing you'll need to worry about is looking after your pot plants, which can always be hooked up to a *sistema de rega semi-automática* – a big container of water with spidery hosepipes running off to all your pots, keeping them drip-fed until you come back.

For those of you planning to cultivate a plot with a bit more greenery, ask yourself what you want it to do for you, and what your limitations are. Is it ornamental or do you want to be able to add ice and a slice of your very own lemons to your afternoon *gin tônica*? What's the temperature range in your area? How much of the year are you going to spend there, and is there anyone nearby you can persuade to pop over and do some watering now and then for you?

Peer over the fence and see how your neighbours use their gardens. What are they growing? You may be able to do more than you think, even if you're not there to water and weed regularly. Some fruit trees survive remarkably well in poor, dry soil and produce a lovely crop – the *amendoeira* (almond) or *oliveira* (olive) for instance, or perhaps a citrus tree – a *laranjeira* (orange) or a *limoeiro* (lemon). How about a *vinha* (grape vine)?

For most Brits in Portugal, the most important parts of the garden are not the lawn and the veg plot, but the swimming pool and the patio. Lazy afternoons by the pool and summer evenings sipping a glass of the local *vinho* and eating olives on the patio with friends. Isn't that why you bought the place?

Check at the câmara

- Walls and fences may be subject to planning controls. If you want to build a substantial one, you may need approval.
- A swimming pool will also need planning approval – and may well increase your local taxes.

As cercas – walls, fences and hedges

If you have bought a plot of land, the only thing marking it off from your neighbours may be a line in the sand – literally! While we're all for being friendly with the people next door, you will probably want something more substantial than that. As a general rule, you can create any kind of *cerca* (enclosure) up to 1 m high without planning permission, but there are exceptions.

The best way to start – as always – it to look around you. What do the locals have around their properties? Would this suit you? If so, you can almost certainly go ahead without worrying. If you want to build something that is very different, go and talk to the *câmara* first.

balaustrada (f)	stone balustrade
bambu (m)	bamboo
cerca (f)	any kind of enclosure – wall, fence or hedge
malha (f)	mesh fencing
muro (m)	wall (stone)
painel (m) de vedação	fencing panel
portão (m)	gate
poste (m)	fence post
sebe (m)	hedge
vedação (f)	fence

Os anexos – outbuildings

When planning outbuildings, remember that if they are anything more than a big dog kennel or a small tool store *uma licença de obras* (building permit) is probably needed

A piscina – the swimming pool

For many people, a swimming pool is an essential part of any home in the sun. Installing one is quite simple – just decide how big it should be, where it should go and how much you are willing to pay, then get a professional to do the job! It won't be cheap – expect to pay at least €15,000 for a decent-sized pool – and it will need regular maintenance, which will take time and money. But the pool will add value to the house, if you ever come to resell it, and you cannot put a price on the pleasure it will give to you and your guests.

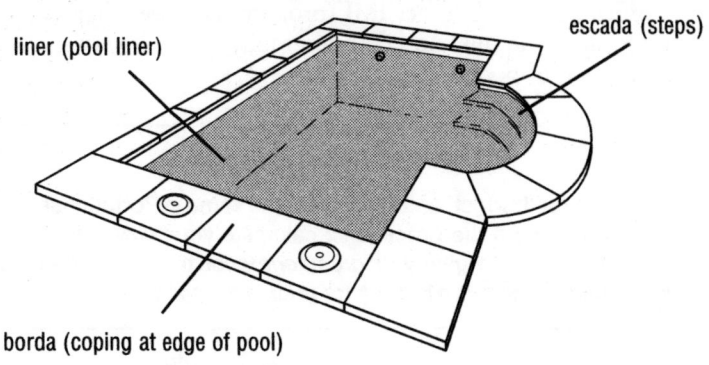

liner (pool liner)

escada (steps)

borda (coping at edge of pool)

Some things to consider when planning your pool – discuss these with the pool builder:

- Should you opt for salt water pool? Salt water discourages algae and needs lower chlorine levels, but can corrode metal pipes and machinery.

- What kind of summer and winter covers will the pool need? Can you haul a plastic cover off by hand or will you need a roller? Or how about a *cobertura telescópica* – a glazed roof on runners which slides open or closed as needed?

- Where will the pump and filtration unit go? Is there a good place in the outbuildings or do you need a pump house?

- How big, and what shape? Curved pools are more expensive but are easier to clean – no corners to stymie robot cleaners.

- Do you want a pre-formed pool liner or a custom-made concrete structure? What will you cover it with – pool paint, ceramic tiles or mosaic?

The cost of a pool can vary enormously, so many of these questions are best left until you've answered the first and most important ones: what's your *orçamento* (budget)? Who will use it, for what, and how often?

Make sure you or your builders get a *licença de obras* (building permit) for the pool – unless it's a *piscina inflatável* (temporary inflatable pool). If you get your pool builders involved early in the process, they can guide you through the paperwork, or even handle it for you completely.

If you construct a fixed pool, you must inform the local *finanças* (tax office), as it will affect IMI (property tax, see Chapter 2). Don't forget to do this. Aerial photography makes it very simple to keep track of pools!

Budgets and quotes

The word for 'budget' and 'quote' are the same in Portuguese – *orçamento*. So the process is: calculate your *orçamento*, get a few firms to give you *orçamentos* for the work, then see which *orçamento* is best for your *orçamento*. Got it?

algicida (f)	anti-algal product
azulejos (mpl)	tiles
bomba (f)	pump
borda (f)	edge of pool
cerca de segurança (f)	safety fence
cloro (m)	chlorine
cobertura (f)	cover
escada (f)	steps
filtro (m) de areia	sand filter
limpador (m) de piscina automático	pool cleaning robot
liner (m)	pool liner
pastilhas (fpl)	mosaic tiles
pavimento (m) de madeira	decking
piscina (f)	pool
piscina de betão	concrete-built pool

piscina inflatável	inflatable pool
piscina prefabricada	moulded pool liner
tinta (f) de piscinas	pool-lining paint
tratamentos químicos (mpl)	chemical treatments

Pool robots come in weird and wonderful shapes, but all work in much the same way. They are powered by the main pump and wander across the bottom and up the sides, dislodging and hoovering up sediment.

Os móveis do jardim – garden furniture

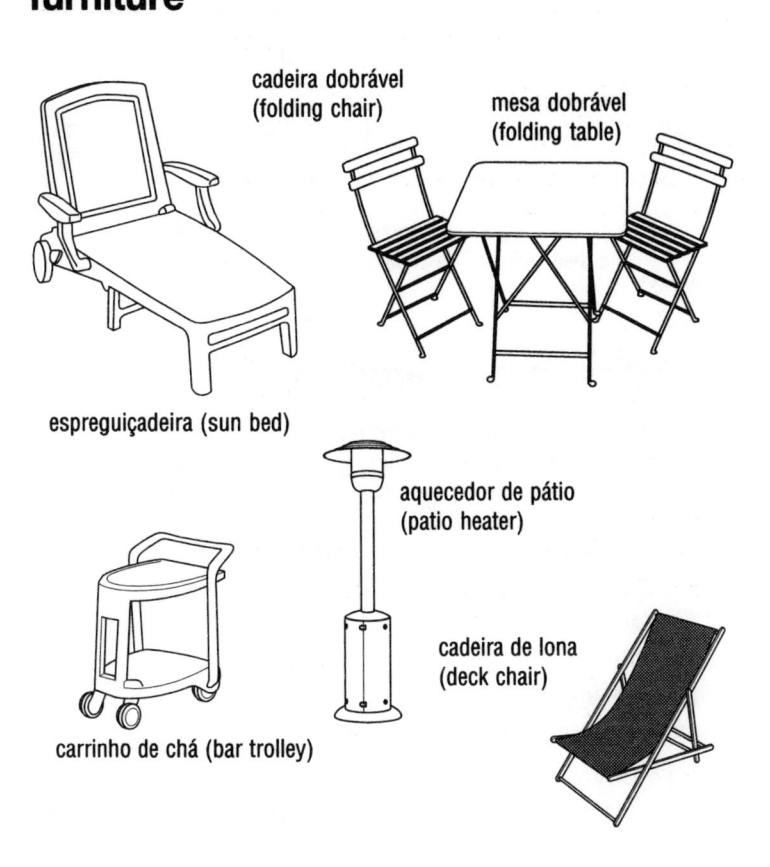

cadeira dobrável (folding chair)

mesa dobrável (folding table)

espreguiçadeira (sun bed)

aquecedor de pátio (patio heater)

cadeira de lona (deck chair)

carrinho de chá (bar trolley)

alumínio (m)	aluminium
almofada (f)	cushion
aquecedor de pátio (m)	patio heater
baloiço (m)	swing seat
cadeira de lona (f)	deck chair
cadeira dobrável (f)	folding chair
caixa (f) de areia	sand pit
candeeiro de jardim (m)	garden light
carrinho de chá (m)	bar trolley
churrasqueira (f)	barbeque
colchão (de espreguiçadeira)	mattress (for sun bed)
espreguiçadeira (f)	sun bed
ferro fundido (m)	cast iron
guarda-sol (m)	sunshade
luz de segurança (f)	security light
rede (m)	hammock

A *luz de energia solar* stores electricity during the day and then switches on at dusk to shine all night.

A jardinagem – gardening

Garden centres are not as common in Portugal as they are in the UK – traditionally, urbanites live in garden-less apartments, while in the countryside cultivating land is a job, not a hobby. However, enough people have small gardens or extensive pot plant collections these days, so you should be able to find somewhere which stocks plants and seeds, pots, composts, tools and so on.

- The larger *bricolagens* (DIY stores) usually have a gardening section.

- In rural areas there are agricultural retailers who also handle gardening supplies. These can be very good value.

- If you want trees and shrubs, go to the *viveiro* (nursery).

Ervas aromáticas and ervas daninhas

Uma erva is a herb, but in a wider sense, the word can refer to pretty much anything small and green. *Ervas aromáticas* are cooking herbs, but watch out for *ervas daninhas* ('harmful herbs'), which are weeds.

cebolhina (f)	chives
coentro (m)	coriander
endro (m)	dill
funcho (m)	fennel
hortelã (f)	mint
manjerição (m)	basil
manjerona (f)	marjoram
oregãos (mpl)	oregano
salsa (f)	parsley
tomilho (m)	thyme

Water, water, nowhere...

Given the arid summers in many parts of Portugal, there are plenty of ingenious water-efficient devices for watering on the market. Look for *rega gota a gota* (drip watering) systems, and make sure they're *automático* if you're not around much. Many systems can be linked to a *sensor de chuva* (rain sensor) which cuts off the water supply when it's not needed.

As ferramentas – tools

abrigo de jardim (m)	garden shed
adubo (m)	fertiliser
aspersor (m)	sprinkler
barril (m)	water barrel
carrinho (m) de mão	wheelbarrow – not a reference to the gardening habits of Chinese communists! *carrinho* is a small cart, *de mão* means 'for the hand'

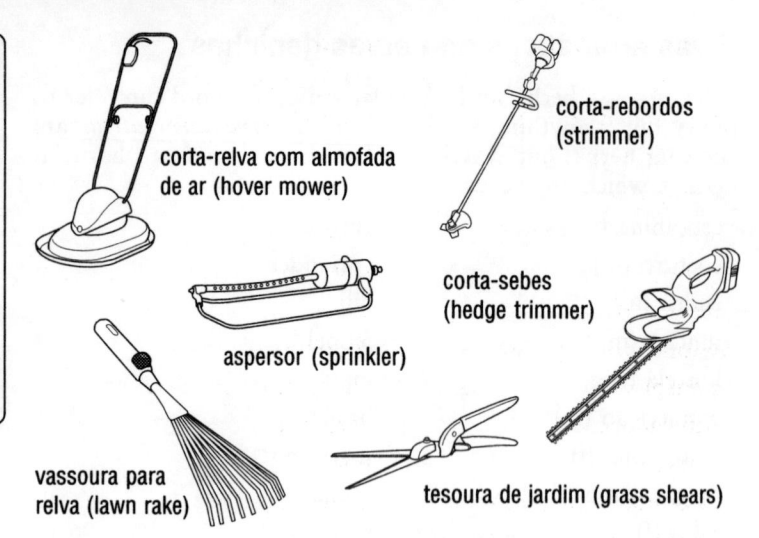

corta-relva com almofada de ar (hover mower)

corta-rebordos (strimmer)

corta-sebes (hedge trimmer)

aspersor (sprinkler)

vassoura para relva (lawn rake)

tesoura de jardim (grass shears)

chafariz (m)	fountain
colher de jardineiro (m)	potting trowel
com motor	motorised
corta-rebordos (m)	strimmer
corta-relva (m)	mower
… com almofada de ar	hover mower
corta-sebes (m)	hedge trimmer
electroserra (f)	chain saw
enrolador (m)	roller for hosepipe
escarifador (m)	scarifier
estufa (f)	greenhouse
extensão (f)	extension lead
floreira (f)	planter (the rectangular pot, not the person who plants!)
forquilha (f)	gardening fork
incinerador (m)	incinerator
mangueira (f)	hose
microtrator (m)	ride-on mower (literally 'micro-tractor')
pá (f)	spade
pá de transplantar	potting trowel

pequeno lago (m)	pond
rega (f)	watering, irrigation
rega gota a gota (f)	drop-by-drop watering system
relvado (m)	lawn
semente (f)	seed
sensor (m) de chuva	rain sensor
terra (f)	soil
tesoura (f) de jardim	shears
tesoura (f) de podar	secateurs
transplantador (m)	transplanting trowel
trituradora (f)	shredder
vaso (m)	pot
vassoura (f) de jardim	garden brush
vassoura para relva (f)	lawn rake

English – Portuguese quick reference

Walls, fences and hedges – as cercas

enclosure (any kind)	cerca (f)
fence	vedação (f)
fence post	poste (m)
fencing panel	painel (m) de vedação
gate	portão (m)
hedge	sebe (m)
mesh fencing	malha (f)
wall	muro (m)

Swimming pool – a piscina

chlorine	cloro (m)
cover	cobertura (f)
decking	pavimento (m) de madeira
edge of pool	borda (f)
glass mosaic tiling	pastilhas (fpl) de vidro

pool liner, moulded	piscina prefabricada (f)
pool liner, sheet	liner (m)
pool paint	tinta (f) de piscinas
pump	bomba (f)
safety fence	cerca de segurança (f)
sand filter	filtro (m) de areia
steps	escada (f)
tiles	azulejos (mpl)

Garden furniture – os móveis do jardim

aluminium	alumínio (m)
bar trolley	carrinho de chá (m)
cushion	almofada (f)
deck chair	cadeira de lona (f)
folding	dobrável (adj)
garden light	candeeiro de jardim (f)
mattress for sun bed	colchão (m) de espreguiçadeira
parasol chauffant	aquecedor (m) de pátio
sand pit	caixa (f) de areia
security light	luz de segurança (f)
sun bed	espreguiçadeira (f)
swing seat	baloiço (m)

Cooking herbs – as ervas aromáticas

basil	manjerição (m)
chives	cebolhina (f)
coriander	coentro (m)
dill	endro (m)
fennel	funcho (m)
marjoram	manjerona (f)
mint	hortelã (f)

oregano	oregãos (mpl)
parsley	salsa (f)
thyme	tomilho (m)

Gardening – a jardinagem

almond tree	amendoeira (f)
extension lead	extensão (f)
fertiliser	adubo (m)
fountain	chafariz (m)
garden brush	vassoura (f) de jardim
garden shed	abrigo (m) de jardim
gardening fork	forquilha (f)
grape vine	vinha (f)
greenhouse	estufa (f)
hedge trimmer	corta-sebes (m)
hose	mangueira (f)
hover mower	corta-relva com almofada de ar
incinerator	incinerador (m)
lawn	relvado (m)
lawn rake	vassoura para relva (f)
lemon tree	limoeiro (m)
mower	corta-relva (m)
olive tree	oliveiro (m)
orange tree	laranjeira (f)
pot	vaso (m)
potting trowel	pá (f) de transplantar
rake	ancinho (m)
ride-on mower	microtrator (m)
roller (for hosepipe)	enrolador (m)
seed	semente (f)
shears	tesoura (f) de jardim

shredder	trituradora (f)
soil	terra (f)
spade	pá (f)
sprinkler	aspersor (m)
strimmer	corta-rebordos (m)
water barrel	barril (m)
wheelbarrow	carrinho (f) de mão

10 uma hora de português – an hour of Portuguese

The CD and the book

This chapter and the CD are built around the same sets of words, and should be used together. The CD gives practice in speaking and listening; the book links the written to the spoken word.

The aim of this chapter is not to teach you Portuguese – if you want to learn the language properly, try one of the titles in the *Teach Yourself* series, such as *Portuguese* or *Instant Portuguese*. The aim here is to provide you with a core of words and phrases that will help you to find what you need when you are buying, building, maintaining or equipping your Portuguese home.

If you already speak Portuguese to a greater or lesser degree, we hope that this chapter will give you a firmer grasp of those specialist words that the householder needs. Skip the rest of this section and go straight to *A pesquisa – the search* (page 162) and Track 2 on the CD.

Speaking and listening

When you speak Portuguese to a native, don't try too hard to get a perfect accent. If the Portuguese think that you can speak their language well, they won't make allowances when they talk to you. And you need them to make allowances! Portuguese has some unfamiliar sounds in it and takes a while to get used to – you need them to slow down so that you can distinguish each word or phrase from the next. Rehearse what you want to say, in your head, let it flow out smoothly, then stand there like an idiot after they reply, without a clue as to what they said. I've done this too often myself!

Speak slowly yourself, and let them hear from your accent that you are a foreigner, and they might speak more slowly and clearly to you. If not, you might have to ask them to slow down.

Here's your first – and most essential – Portuguese phrase:

outra vez, e mais devagar   again and more slowly

To which you could add, politely:

por favor   please

What follows is a brief guide to basic pronunciation. Listen to the CD while you are working through this.

Lost consonants

The Portuguese do not pronounce every letter. *h* is always silent and when a word ends in *m* or *ns* the last *m* or *n* is turned into a kind of nasal sound instead. When a word ends in *l*, the *l* sounds more like a **w**.

Portuguese	sounds like	means
bem	**bay(n)**	good
homens	**o-may(n)sh**	men
Portugal	**portoogow**	Portugal

Other consonants

Most are pronounced as in English. These aren't.

c is **k** if followed by another consonant, or by *a*, *o* or *u*

cobre   **kobry**   copper

c is **s** if followed by *e* or *i*, or if it written *ç*

| *bacia* | **baseeya** | bowl |
| *terça-feira* | **tairsa-fairuh** | Tuesday |

ch is **sh**

chaminé   **shamminay**   chimney

g is like our **g** in 'garden' unless followed by *e* or *i*, when it sounds like the **s** in 'pleasure'

garagem   **gararzhem**   garage

l between a vowel and a consonant, or after a vowel at the end of a word, sounds more like a **w**

| *altura* | **owtoora** | height |
| *beiral* | **bayrow** | eaves |

lh is **ly** as in 'million'

colher   **colyair**   trowel

nh is **ny** as in 'onion'

senhor   **senyor**   mister

qu before *e* or *i* is pronounced **k**, not **kw**

quinze   **kinze**   fifteen

But before *a* and *o*, *qu* is pronounced **kw**

quatro   **kwatro**   four

r at the start of a word is slightly trilled

| *roupa* | **rropa** | clothes |

rr is a heavy, aspirated **h**, like the French **r**

| *terra* | **ter-ha** | earth |

s is a soft **s** as in 'sun', except when it's between two vowels – then it becomes hard like our **z** – or at the end of words, where it is usually a **sh** as in 'sugar'

sofá	**so-fah**	sofa
mesa	**mayza**	table
portas	**portash**	doors

x has several slightly different forms in different situations, but it normally sounds like **sh** as in 'sugar'

| *caixa* | **kyshah** | box |

z sounds like our **z**, except at the end of a word, when it sounds like the **s** in 'pleasure'

| *verniz* | **vairneezh** | varnish |

Vowels

First, the vowels by themselves:

a is **a** as in 'father'

| *casa* | **caza** | house |

e is usually **e** as in 'hey', but changes at the ends of words. If the word ends in *t* or *d* – it's like a tiny **uh** sound. At the end of other words, it sounds like the **i** in 'going'.

pedra	**peydra**	stone
mármore	**marmorey**	marble
parede	**pared(uh)**	wall

i is **ee** as in 'meet'

| *pintar* | **peentar** | to paint |

o is **o** as in 'copper', except at the end of a word, when it is **oo** as in 'move' instead

| *onde* | **ond(uh)** | where |
| *granito* | **graneetoo** | granite |

u is **oo** as in 'move'

| *tubo* | **tooboo** | tube |

When two vowels appear next to each other, they are often run together, as with the following:

ai is **i** as in 'file'

   mais   **meyesh**   more

ei is **ey** as in 'they'

   pedreiro   **pedrayroo**   bricklayer

oi is **oy** as in 'boy'

   clarabóia   **klaraboya**   skylight

ou is **o** as in 'old'

   tesoura   **tezowra**   scissors

Finally, there are the nasal sounds which make Portuguese so distinctive. There are two main places these occur – vowels in the middle of words when they are followed by *n* and then another consonant, and vowels with the squiggly accent (called a *til*).

   jantar   **zha(n)tar**   to dine
   conjunto   **co(n)zhoo(n)too**   set (as in a set of spanners)

ão is a nasal **ow**, as if you were saying 'now' with a heavy cold

   chão   **shaow**   floor

ãe is a nasal **i** as in 'file' (but with a cold)

   alemães   **alem-eye(n)sh**   Germans

õe is a nasal **oy** as in 'boy' (but with a cold)

   fundações   **fu(n)da-soy(n)sh**   foundations

Gender and endings

All nouns are either masculine or feminine. We've never understood why or what determines the gender of a noun (apart from the obvious ones that refer to people or animals). One that ends in *a* is almost certainly feminine, as are most words ending in *ção*, but that leaves an awful lot that you just have to know.

A noun's gender affects the words around it. For 'the' you use *o* if the noun is masculine and *a* if it is feminine; likewise 'a' is either *um* (m) or *uma* (f). If there's more than one of them, it's *os* (m) or *as* (f) for 'the' and *uns* (m) or *umas* (f) for 'some'.

For example, *casa* (house) is feminine, and *andar* (apartment) is masculine. That gives us:

the house	*a casa*
the apartment	*o andar*
a house	*uma casa*
an apartment	*um andar*
the houses	*as casas*
the apartments	*os andares*
some houses	*umas casas*
some apartments	*uns andares*

Try not to get too hung up on the gender thing. If you talk about *o casa*, instead of *a casa*, a Portuguese person will know what you mean.

Adjectives have a different ending if a noun is masculine or feminine. Usually, it's just a matter of swapping the final *o* for an *a*. For example, *pequeno* means 'small', so 'a small house' – which is feminine – becomes *uma casa pequena* (the adjective is usually placed after the noun).

Sometimes it doesn't change at all, as with *grande* (big) for example – you can have *um andar grande* (a big apartment) or *uma casa grande* (a big house).

The endings of adjectives also change with plural nouns – and usually by just adding an *s* to the end, to match the *s* on the end of the noun.

a small house	*uma casa pequena*
the small houses	*as casas pequenas*
the big apartments	*os andares grandes*

Verbs

Portuguese verbs 'conjugate'. Their endings, and sometimes the whole word, change depending upon who is doing the thing and when they are doing it. Verbs also conjugate in English, but not as much. However, there's a bright side – as the endings of words are often not pronounced, they may be spelled differently but sound the same.

For example, *falar* means 'to speak'. Here's how it conjugates:

eu falo	**eyoo fahloo**	I speak
tu falas	**too fahlas**	you speak (informal)
você fala	**vossay fahla**	you speak (polite)
ele fala	**elly fahla**	he speaks
ela fala	**ella fahla**	she speaks
nós falamos	**nosh fahlamoosh**	we speak
vocês falam	**vossash fahlow(n)**	you speak (plural)
eles falam	**elysh fahlow(n)**	they speak (male)
elas falam	**elash fahlow(n)**	they speak (female)

Notice that the verb is the same for many of them – there's actually only four different forms. That makes life simple, and in practice if you said *você falam* to a Portuguese shopkeeper, they would know what you meant well enough to sell you stuff. To make things even easier, I'd recommend ignoring the *tu* form for the moment too (see box below). You'll be dealing with people you don't know that well, so the polite *você* form will be much more appropriate.

Tu o você – which you?

Confusingly, the Portuguese have four words for 'you'. *Tu* and *você* are for when you are talking to one person, but *tu* is used with people you are very close to, while *você* shows more respect. *Vós* is the plural version of *tu*, but is hardly ever used these days. *Vocês* is the plural version of *você*.

The Portuguese also use *o senhor* and *a senhora* to mean 'you'. This is the way we imply great respect by using the third person: 'Would sir/madam like to see the menu...?' but in Portugal it is much more normal. When in doubt, use *você* or *vocês* – it's the easiest way!

The only thing you need to watch out for when listening to Portuguese is that they often drop the personal pronouns (I, you, we, he, she, etc). Because all their verb forms sound different, they don't really need them in a sentence. When you are speaking you might want to keep them in to avoid misunderstandings.

Most other verbs that end *ar* conjugate in the same way, so to say these, just chop off the *ar* and add *o* for the 'I' form, *amos* for the 'we' form, and then *a* for any other singular form, or *am* for any other plural form.

e.g. with *pintar* (to paint), you would say:

eu pinto	-o	I paint
nós pintamos	-amos	we paint
ele/ela/você pinta	-a	he/she/you paint(s)
eles/elas/vocês pintam	-am	they/you paint

Other verbs end in *er* or *ir*. Likewise with these, trim the verb down to its core and add similar endings:

viver	-er	to live
eu vivo	-o	I live
nós vivemos	-imos	we live
ele/ela/você vive	-e	he/she/you live(s)
eles/elas/vocês vivem	-em	they/you live
unir	-ir	to join
eu uno	-o	I join
nós unimos	-imos	we join
ele/ela/você une	-e	he/she/you join(s)
eles/elas/vocês unem	-em	they/you join

Some verbs change more. You should at least be aware of these.

ser – **to be**

eu sou	**eyoo sew**	I am
tu és	**too ess**	you are (informal)
ele/ela é	**elly/ella eh**	he/she is
nós somos	**nosh somoosh**	we are
você é	**vossay eh**	you are (formal)
eles/elas são	**elysh/elash sow(n)**	they are
vocês são	**vossaysh sow(n)**	you are (formal)

ter – **to have**

eu tenho	**eyoo tey(n)yoo**	I have
tu tens	**too tey(n)sh**	you have (informal)
ele/ela tem	**elly/ella tey(n)**	he/she has
nós temos	**nosh temoosh**	we have
você tem	**vossay tey(n)**	you have (formal)
eles/elas têm	**elysh/elash taay(n)**	they have
vocês têm	**vossaysh taay(n)**	you have (formal)

We've only looked at the present tense. There are also several ways of talking about past and future events, all of which affect the shape and sound of the verb. And there is no single pattern to the way they conjugate, even for the 'regular' verbs – there are dozens of patterns and permutations in total. Take my advice, live in the present, never write anything down, and just chop off the ending of the verb and add *-amos* or *-imos* for *nós*, *-o* for *eu*, and *-a* or *-e* for everything else. It's not perfect, but you'll get by and you will amuse the locals. When they've stopped laughing, they'll be pleased to help you – at least you're trying, which is more than can be said of many of our fellow Brits abroad.

ser e estar – to be or to be!

Another thing which can cause confusion is that the Portuguese also have two words for 'to be'. *Ser* is used mainly to describe permanent properties of a thing, e.g. *A casa é bonita* (the house is pretty). *Estar* is used mainly in relation to temporary positions and conditions, e.g. *Os pregos estão ali* – the nails are over there – or *O telhado está em boa condição* – the roof is in good condition (for now!). It won't matter much if you get it wrong yourself, but it's good to be aware of when you hear other people using *ser* or *estar*.

não... – not

To say 'not' you just add *não* before the verb. For example:

   I am not...   *eu não sou...*

Here's a 'not' phrase you may find very useful.

   I do not understand   *não compreendo*

If you want to say 'not' without a verb, it's the same word:

   not many   *não muito*

'This house sells itself'

We've come across the expression *vende-se esta casa* already, meaning 'this house is for sale'. In fact, the literal translation is 'this house sells itself'. Some common phrases you'll meet in this book use this kind of structure. For example:

   Do you sell nails?   *vendem-se aqui pregos?*

Literally: 'do nails sell themselves here?' – or, in better English, 'are nails sold here?'

The important thing to note is that the verb in these sentences does not refer to the 'I' or 'you' in the English, but to the thing you are looking for. This means it has to change for singular and plural objects:

>Is this hammer for sale?   *Vende-se este martelo?*
>Are these screws for sale?   *Vendem-se estos parafusos?*

Having said that, don't get hung up on matching the verb perfectly – if you say *vende-se aqui os pregos?* nobody's going to mind!

Greetings

hello, literally 'good day'	*bom dia*
good evening	*boa tarde*
goodbye	*até logo*
thank you (said by a man)	*obrigado*
thank you (said by a woman)	*obrigada*
don't mention it	*de nada*
excuse me	*desculpe*
how do you do?	*como está?*
fine, thanks	*bem, obrigado/a*
I am called...	*eu chamo-me...*

Asking questions

To form questions, just say it as if it was a statement, but with a rising inflection:

>do you speak English?   *você fala inglês?*
>is the house pretty?   *a casa é bonita?*

Questions mainly use the same order as in English, but they don't switch the verb and subject over as often as we do. The subject (the house) usually comes before the verb (is).

quem (who), *onde* (where), *que* (what), *quando* (when) and *porque* (why) questions use the same order as in English.

English	Portuguese
where is the town hall?	*onde é a câmara?*
it's to the right	*é à direita*
it's to the left	*é à esquerda*
go straight on	*va em frente*
it's over there	*é lá*
it's right here	*é aqui mesmo*
how much is it?	*quanto é?*
why?	*porque?*
this house is cheap, why?	*esta casa é barata, porque?*
why is this house so dear?	*porque é tão cara esta casa?*
how old is this house?	*quantos anos tem esta casa?*
what time is it?	*que horas são?*
it is 7 o'clock	*são sete horas*
half past eight	*são oito (horas) e meia*
quarter to ten	*são dez menos um quarto*
7 in the morning	*sete da manhã*
3 in the afternoon	*três da tarde*
it's lunch time	*é a hora do almoço*
when?, at what time?	*a que horas?*

Os números – numbers

1	um/uma*	14	catorze
2	dois/duas*	15	quinze
3	três	16	dezasseis
4	quatro	17	dezassete
5	cinco	18	dezoito
6	seis	19	dezanove
7	sete		
8	oito	20	vinte
9	nove	21	vinte e um/uma*
10	dez	22	vinte e dois/duas*
		...	...
11	onze	30	trinta
12	doze	40	quarenta
13	treze	50	cinquenta

60	sessenta
70	setenta
80	oitenta
90	noventa
100	cem
101	cento e um/uma*
...	...
200	duzentos/as*
300	trezentos/as*
400	quatrocentos/as*
500	quinhientos/as*
...	...
1000	mil
2000	dois mil

* These numbers have masculine/feminine forms

on what day?	*que dia?*
what date?	*que data?*
can we set a date?	*podemos marcar uma data?*

As datas – dates

Os dias – the days

Sunday	domingo
Monday	segunda-feira*
Tuesday	terça-feira*
Wednesday	quarta-feira*
Thursday	quinta-feira*
Friday	sexta-feira*
Saturday	sábado
tomorrow	amanhã
today	hoje
yesterday	ontem

* feira is often left out

As meses – the months

January	janeiro
February	fevereiro
March	março
April	abril
May	maio
June	junho
July	julho
August	agosto
September	setembro
October	outubro
November	novembro
December	dezembro

A pesquisa – the search (Track 2)

Let's start with some words and phrases to help you find that house.

I am looking for...	*procuro...*
we are looking for...	*procuramos...*
I want to buy...	*quero comprar...*
we want to buy...	*queremos comprar...*
...a small apartment	*...um apartamento pequeno*
...a large apartment	*...um apartamento grande*
...a house	*...uma casa*
...in the town	*...na cidade*
...a house in the country	*...uma quinta*
...a villa near the sea	*...uma vivenda perto do mar*

...to restore   *...para renovar*
...in good condition   *...em boa condição*
is this house for sale?   *esta casa está à venda?*

Defining the house

Three key ways to define a house are its size – measured in square metres of floor space – the number of rooms and its price. You'll need to brush up your numbers for all of these. But if you want to make sure that you've understood the numbers correctly, ask the agents to write them down. Figures don't need translation!

about	*aproximadamente*
more than	*mais de*
less than	*menos de*
50 m² (cottage size)	*cinquenta metros quadrados*
100 m² (average UK semi)	*cem metros cuadrados*
200 m² (large detached)	*duzentos metros cuadrados*
two bedrooms	*dois quartos*
five rooms	*cinco divisões*
€60 000	*sessenta mil euros*
€120 000	*cento e vinte mil euros*
€1 000 000	*um milhão de euros*

The features

What features are essential, desirable or to be avoided?

there must be...	*é preciso...*
is there...	*há...*
is it possible to build...	*é possível construir...*
...a kitchen	*...uma cozinha*
...a bathroom	*...uma casa de banho*
...a swimming pool	*...uma piscina*
...a garden	*...um jardim*
...an attic	*...um sótão*
...a cellar	*...uma cave*
is there a beautiful view?	*tem boa vista?*

does it need work doing?	*precisa de renovação?*
is it on the mains drains?	*está ligado ao esgoto?*
is the roof in a good state?	*o telhado está em boa condição?*

Your decision

And what do you think of the property? Do you want to keep looking or is it time to start negotiating the price?

no, thank you	*não, obrigado/a*
it's too dear	*é demasiado caro*
it's too big/small	*é demasiado grande/pequeno*
there is too much to do	*precisa de demasiada renovação*
perhaps	*pode ser*
there are other houses I have to see	*há outras casas que tenho que ver*
do you have other houses?	*tem outras casas?*
I like this house...	*gosto desta casa...*
we like this house...	*gostamos desta casa...*
...but not the price	*...mais não do preço*
can we negotiate?	*podemos negociar?*
my offer is...	*a minha oferta é...*
it's perfect!	*é perfeito!*
agreed	*está bem*

A venda – the sale (Track 3)

There is not enough in this book to enable you to handle safely the legal and financial aspects of house purchase. You must have a good grasp of Portuguese – and of Portuguese law – or the services of a translator and/or English-speaking lawyer.

Before you commit yourself to the purchase, you may want to check the price, or the cost – and feasibility – of essential works.

could you recommend...	*você pode recomendar...*
...a surveyor	*...um engenheiro*
...an architect	*...um arquitecto*

...a notary	...*um notário*
I need/we need...	*preciso de / precisamos de...*
...a valuation...	...*uma avaliação...*
...an estimate...	...*um orçamento...*
...for this house	...*para esta casa*

(There is more on estimates in the next section, *As obras – building work*, Track 4.)

You might want to find out the level of the local taxes and/or the service charges in an apartment block, and you should also check who's paying the agent's fees.

where is the town hall?	*onde é a câmara?*
where is the tax office?	*onde são as Finanças?*
how much are the taxes for this address?	*quanto são os impostos para este endereço?*
how much are the service charges of the block?	*quais são as despesas de condomínio?*
who pays the agency fees?	*quem paga as commissões do agente?*
the seller pays	*o vendedor paga-as*

With your queries answered, you should be ready to commit, though there may be conditions in some cases.

we are ready to buy	*estamos dispostos a comprar*
I want to buy this house...	*quero comprar esta casa...*
...at the price of €...000	...*pelo preço de...mil euros*
...under these conditions	...*com estas cláusulas de anulação*
there must be a satisfactory planning search	*o parecer da câmara tem que ser satisfatório*
I must get a mortgage	*tenho que obter uma hipoteca*
I would like to see the land registry record	*quero ver a certidão do registo*
I can't pay the deposit today	*não posso pagar o depósito hoje*
I will transfer the money from the UK	*farei uma transferência do Reino Unido*

If you want to clarify any points of the sale agreement, or set up a Portuguese will, you will need to visit the *notário*.

where is the notary's office?	onde é o escritório do notário?
do you speak English?	você fala inglês?
I want to make a will	quero fazer um testamento

If they are present, get the water, gas, electricity and telephone accounts transferred to your name at the time of the sale. Ask your *solicitador*.

which utilities are connected?	que serviços existem?
can you transfer the accounts to us?	você pode transferir as contas para nós?
where is the recycling centre?	onde é o centro de reciclagem?

And don't forget the *por favor* when you ask a question, or the *obrigado/a* when you get a reply.

As obras – building work (Track 4)

As long as you hold your meetings on site, armed with an *esboço* (sketch) or *plano* (plan), you can get a long way with a limited vocabulary and lots of hand waving. First find your work force. Ask at the *agente imobiliário* or the *câmara*.

can you recommend...	você pode recomendar...
...an architect	...um arquitecto
...a builder	...um construtor
...a joiner	...um carpinteiro
...a roofer	...um telhador
...a plumber	...um canalizador
...an electrician	...um electricista

Then specify the job on site. Notice that the word for 'new' is *novo* if the noun is masculine, or *nova* if it is feminine.

here are my sketch and plan	aqui estão o meu esboço e o meu plano
I want...	quero...
...to knock down the walls	...derrubar estas paredes
...to knock down these outbuildings	...derrubar estos anexos
...to make two rooms	...para criar duas divisões
the house needs...	a casa precisa de...

...a new roof	...*um telhado novo*
...a new floor	...*um soalho novo*
I want to build...	*quero construir...*
...a new bathroom	...*uma casa de banho nova*
...a new kitchen	...*uma cozinha nova*
...an extra bedroom	...*um quarto extra*
...a garage	...*uma garagem*
...a swimming pool	...*uma piscina*
this big (with gestures!)	*deste tamanho*
this high	*desta altura*
can you give me an estimate for this work?	*você pode dar-me um orçamento para estas obras?*
when could you do it?	*quando é que você pode fazê-las?*
Do you need planning permission for that?	*é preciso ter uma licença de obras para isso?*
please give me...	*por favor, dême...*
...the town hall's address	...*o endereço da câmara*
...a form for...	...*um formulário para...*
...planning permission	...*uma licença de obras*

A estrutura – the structure

Talking to o construtor – the builder (Track 5)

can you build...	*você pode construir...*
...a brick wall here	...*um muro de tijolos aquí*
...a partition wall	...*uma parede interior alí*
...a stone fireplace	...*uma lareira de pedra*
...a reinforced concrete floor	...*um soalho de betão armado*
can you...	*você pode...*
...strengthen the foundations	... *fortalecer as fundações*
...mend this crack	...*reparar esta racha*
there is rising damp	*há humidade nas paredes*
the house needs a damp course	*a casa precisa dum isolante da humidade*

Finding tools and materials at the bricolagem (Track 6)

where can I find...	*onde posso encontrar...*
...builder's tools	*...as ferramentas de construção*
...a bucket	*...um balde*
...a wood chisel	*...um formão*
...a filling knife	*...uma espátula*
...a shavehook	*...um raspador*
...a shovel	*...uma pá*
...a spirit level	*...um nível de bolha*
...a trowel	*...um colher*
...breeze blocks	*...os blocos de cimento*
...bricks	*...os tijolos*
...insulation panels	*...os paineis isolantes*
...plaster blocks	*...os blocos de gesso*
...cement	*...o cimento*
...a lintel	*...uma verga*
...a plasterboard panel	*...as placas de gesso*
...sand	*...a areia*
...stones	*...as pedras*
...treatments for mould	*...os productos contra o mofo*
where can I hire a concrete mixer?	*onde posso alugar uma betoneira?*

Talking to o carpinteiro and o telhador – the carpenter and the roofer (Track 7)

I would like...	*quero...*
...to create a terrace roof	*...construir um terraço no telhado*
can you build...	*você pode construir...*
...a lathe and plaster ceiling	*...um tecto de ripado rebocado*
can you install...	*você pode instalar...*
...a skylight	*...uma clarabóia*
...lining felt	*...o papel-feltro betuminado*
...insulation	*...o isolamento*

can you renovate...	*você pode renovar...*
...these rafters	*...estas asnas*
...the joists	*...as vigas*
...the roof trusses	*...a amarração do telhado*
...a hip roof	*...um telhado a quatro águas*
...the roof timbers	*...os caibros*
...the lathing	*...o ripado*
...the ridge	*...a cumeeira*
...the flashing	*...a chapa*
...the slate clips	*...os pregos de ardósia*
oak or pine?	*de carvalho o de pinho?*
a roof of...	*um telhado de...*
...flat tiles	*...telhas planas*
...curved tiles	*...telhas de canudo*
...wood	*...madeira*
...slates	*...ardósia*
...thatch	*...colmo*

A carpintaria – woodwork

Talking to o carpinteiro – the joiner (Track 8)

here, we would like...	*aqui, queremos...*
...a built-in cupboard	*...um armário embutido*
...a door	*...uma porta*
...panelling	*...o lambris*
there, we would like...	*ali, queremos...*
...three shelves	*...três prateleiras*
...wood flooring	*...um soalho de madeira*
...a letter box	*...uma caixa de correio*
can you make...	*você pode fazer...*
...a French window	*...uma porta-janela*
...a skylight	*...uma clarabóia*
...new shutters	*...umas persianas novas*

...a roller shutter	...*uma persiana enrolável*
...a slatted shutter	...*uma persiana*
...a spiral staircase	...*uma escada em espiral*
...a new handrail	...*um corrimão novo*
...a fitted wardrobe	...*um guarda-roupa embutido*
...a bookcase	...*uma estante de livros*

Finding materials at the bricolagem (Track 9)

do you have...	*tem...*
...chipboard	*... aglomerado*
...hardboard	*... platex*
...melamine panels	*... paineis laminados*
...veneer	*... folheado*
...plywood	*... contraplacado*
...tongue and grooved wood	*... madeira de encaixe macho/fêmea*
...veneered panels	*... paineis folheados*
...wood panels	*... paineis de madeira*
...hardware for doors	*... ferragens para portas*
...bolts	*... fechos*
...cylinder locks	*... fechaduras de cilindro*
...door handles	*... maçanetas*
...hinges	*... dobradiças*
...split hinges	*... dobradiças macho/fêmea*
...mortice locks	*... fechaduras para embutir*
...latches	*... trincos*

Finding tools at the bricolagem (Track 10)

where are the wood tools?	*onde estão as ferramentas de carpintaria?*
do you sell...	*vende-se /vendem-se aqui...*
...sandpaper	*...lixa*
...chisels	*...formões*
...cutters (Stanley knives)	*...facas universais*
...drill bits	*...brocas*

... electric drills	...*berbequins*
... electric jig saws	...*serras de recortes*
... electric screwdrivers	...*aparafusadoras*
...hammers	...*martelos*
...nails	...*pregos*
...pincers	...*turqueses*
...saws	...*serrotes*
...screws	...*parafusos*
...screwdrivers	...*chaves de fenda*
...tape measures	...*fitas métricas*
...wood glue	...*cola de madeira*

A canalização – plumbing

Talking to o canalizador – the plumber (Track 11)

can you install...	*você pode instalar...*
...gutters	...*as canaleiras*
...some copper pipes	...*umas bichas de cobre*
...a waste water system	...*os tubos de descarga*
...a new joint	...*uma união nova*
...a bath and basin	...*uma banheira e um lavatório*
...a WC	...*uma sanita*
...a septic tank	...*uma fossa séptica*
...soakaway pipes	...*umas valas de infiltração*
where is...	*onde é...*
...the stop cock	...*a válvula de fechamento*
...the drain cock	...*a válvula de descarga*
...the regulator	...*o reductor de pressão*
...the water meter	...*o contador de água*
Help, there's a leak!	*Socorro, há uma fuga de água!*

Shopping for bathroom and kitchen equipment (Track 12)

where can I find...	*onde posso encontrar...*

...basins	...*os lavatórios, as bacias*
...bathtubs	...*as banheiras*
...medicine cabinets	...*os armários de remédios*
...mirrors	...*os espelhos*
...a mixer tap	...*uma torneira misturadora*
...a plug	...*uma tampa*
...a rubbish bin	...*um balde de lixo*
...showers	...*os duches*
...taps	...*as torneiras*
...towel rails	...*os toalheiros*
...a washer	...*uma anilha*
...kitchen equipment	...*os aparatos de cozinha*
...a bowl	...*uma bacia*
...a dishwasher	...*uma máquina de lavar loiça*
...ovens	...*os fornos*
...a kitchen sink	...*um lava-loiças*
...washing machines	...*as máquinas de lavar roupa*
...work surfaces	...*as bancadas de cozinha*
...a sink with two bowls and one drainer	...*um lava-loiças com duas bacias e um escorredor*

Finding tools at the bricolagem (Track 13)

I am looking for...	*procuro...*
...a spanner	...*uma chave-de-boca*
...an adjustable spanner	...*uma chave-de-boca ajustável*
...a hacksaw	...*uma serra para metais*
...a pipe cutter	...*um corta-tubos*
...a soldering lamp	...*um maçarico de brasagem*

O aquecimento e a electricidade – heating and electricity

Talking to o engenheiro de aquecimento and o electricista – the heating engineer and the electrician (Track 14)

can you install...	*você pode instalar...*
...a fireplace	*...uma lareira*
...a boiler	*...uma caldeira*
...a radiator	*...um radiador*
...a stove	*...uma salamandra*
...central heating...	*...o aquecimento central...*
...gas-fired	*...a gás*
where can I buy...	*onde posso comprar...*
...fuel briquettes	*...briquetes*
...firewood	*...lenha*
can you recommend a chimneysweep?	*você pode recomendar um limpa-chaminés?*
can you rewire the house?	*você pode renovar a instalação eléctrica?*
where is/are...	*onde é/são...*
...the mains switch	*...o disjuntor principal*
...the meter	*...o contador*
...the circuit breakers	*...os disjuntores*
can you fit...	*você pode instalar...*
...a socket	*...uma tomada*
...a fuse box	*...um quadro eléctrico*
...a light switch	*...um interruptor*
...a light socket	*...um suporte de lâmpadas*

Shopping for os electrodomésticos – electrical appliances (Track 15)

where can I find...	*onde posso encontrar...*
...blow heaters	*...os aquecedores sopradores*
...convector heaters	*...os convectores eléctricos*

...electric fires	...*os aquecedores eléctricos*
...cookers	...*os fogões*
...DVD players	...*os leitores DVD*
...food processors	...*os robots de cozinha*
...freezers	...*os congeladores*
...fridges	...*os frigoríficos*
...kettles	...*as chaleiras*
...irons	...*os ferros de engomar*
...telephones	...*os telefones*
...TVs	...*os televisores*
...flat screen TVs	...*os televisores de ecrã plano*
...vacuum cleaners	...*os aspiradores*
...light fittings	...*as lâmpadas*
...a ceiling light	...*um plafond*
...a bedside light	...*um candeeiro de mesa de cabeceira*
...a hanging light	...*um candeeiro de suspensão*
...a wall light	...*um aplique*

A decoração – decorating

Finding materials at the bricolagem (Track 16)

where can I find...	*onde posso encontrar...*
...paint	...*a tinta*
...gloss paint	...*a tinta brilhante*
...masonry paint	...*a tinta para fachadas*
...primer	...*o primário*
...undercoat	...*a subcapa*
...varnish	...*o verniz*
...wood stain	...*a velatura de madeira*
do you sell...	*vende-se/vendem-se aqui...*
...wall coverings	...*revestimentos de paredes*
...textiles, for walls	...*revestimentos texteis*

...cork tiles	...*placas de cortiça*
...wallpaper	...*papel de parede*
...lining paper	...*papel de forro*
...tiles	...*azulejos*
...floor tiles	...*pavimentos*
...mirror tiles	...*azulejos espelhos*

Finding tools at the bricolagem (Track 17)

where can I find...	*onde posso encontrar...*
...a measuring tape	...*uma fita métrica*
...a paper stripper	...*uma raspadeira de papel de paredes*
...a pasting brush	...*uma escova de cola*
...brushes	...*as trinchas*
...paint trays	...*os tabuleiros de pintor*
...rollers	...*os rolos*
...scissors	...*uma tesoura*
...a sponge	...*uma esponja*
...string	...*cordel*
...wallpaper paste	...*cola de tapeceiro*
...a wallpaper brush	...*uma escova seca*
...a tile cutter	...*um corta-azulejos*
...wall tiles	...*os azulejos de parede*

Finding floor coverings, curtains and furniture (Track 18)

do you sell...	*vende-se/vendem-se aqui...*
...carpets	...*carpetes*
...rugs	...*tapetes*
...laminate flooring	...*pavimento flutuante*
...vinyl flooring	...*revestimento de vinil*
...wood flooring	...*parquete*
...blinds	...*estores*
...curtains	...*cortinas*
...curtain tracks	...*calhas de cortinas*

...net curtains	...*cortinas de tule*
we are looking for...	*procuramos...*
...an armchair	...*uma poltrona*
...chairs	...*cadeiras*
...a table	...*uma mesa*
...a bookcase	...*uma estante de livros*
...a cupboard	...*um armário*
...a sofa-bed	...*um sofá-cama*
...a bed	...*uma cama*
...a bedside cabinet	...*uma mesa de cabeceira*
...a chest of drawers	...*uma cómoda*
...a wardrobe	...*um guarda-roupa*
...duvets	...*um edredon*
...a mattress	...*um colchão*
...pillows	...*almofadas*

O jardim – the garden

Talking to os construtores – the builders (Track 19)

can you build...	*vocês podem construir...*
...a panelled fence	...*uma vedação de paineis*
...a gate	...*um portão*
...a wall	...*um muro*
...a swimming pool...	...*uma piscina...*
...with a moulded liner	...*com liner prefabricado*
the pool needs...	*a piscina precisa ...*
...coping (for edge of pool)	...*duma borda*

'needs' is *precisa de* but *de* gets rolled into *uma* to become *duma*

...a cover	...*duma cobertura*
...a pump	...*duma bomba*
...a safety fence	...*duma cerca de segurança*
...a sand filter	...*dum filtro de areia*
...some steps	...*duma escada*

Shopping for o jardim – the garden (Track 20)

where can I find...	*onde posso encontrar...*
...deck chairs	*...cadeiras de lona*
...folding chairs	*...cadeiras dobráveis*
...garden lights	*...candeeiros de jardim*
...a patio heater	*...um aquecedor de pátio*
...a sand pit	*...uma caixa de areia*
...a sun bed	*...uma espreguiçadeira*
...a security light	*...uma luz de segurança*
...an extension lead	*...uma extensão eléctrica*
...a garden brush	*...uma vassoura de jardim*
...a hedge trimmer	*...um corta-sebes*
...a hose	*...uma mangueira*
...an incinerator	*...um incinerador*
...mowers	*...corta-relvas*
...potting trowels	*...pás de transplantar*
...rakes	*...ancinhos*
...a ride-on mower	*...um microtrator*
...a roller for a hosepipe	*...um enrolador para mangueiras*
...a sprinkler	*...um aspersor*
...a water barrel	*...um barril*
...seeds	*...as sementes*
...shears	*...uma tesoura de jardim*

| teach yourself | **portuguese phrasebook**
sue tyson-ward |

- Are you going abroad on holiday or business?
- Do you want to look up words quickly and easily?
- Would you like help with your pronunciation?

Portuguese Phrasebook will give you all the words and phrases you need to get you out of trouble, fast. From hotels to hospitals, the book covers all eventualities and the pronunciation guide and alphabetical dictionary are quick and easy to use.

| teach yourself | **beginner's portuguese** |
| | sue tyson-ward |

- Are you new to language learning?
- Do you want lots of practice and examples?
- Do you want to improve your confidence to speak?

Beginner's Portuguese is written for the complete beginner who wants to move at a steady pace and have lots of opportunity to practise. The grammar is explained clearly and does not assume that you have studied a language before. You will learn everything you need to get the most out of a holiday or to go on to further study.

teach yourself

world cultures: portugal
sue tyson-ward

- Are you interested in the story of Portugal and the Portuguese?
- Do you want to understand how the country works today?
- Are you planning a visit to Portugal or learning Portuguese?

World Cultures: Portugal will give you a basic overview of Portugal – the country, its language, its people and its culture – and will enrich any visit or course of study. Vocabulary lists and 'Taking It Further' sections at the end of every unit will equip you to talk and write confidently about all aspects of Portuguese life.